The Book of Nanak

PENGUIN BOOKS

Penguin Books India Pvt. Ltd, 11 Community Centre, Panchsheel Park,
New Delhi 110 017, India

Penguin Group (USA) Inc., 375 Hudson Street, New York, New York
10014, USA

Penguin Group (Canada), 90 Eglinton Avenue East, Suite 700, Toronto,
Ontario, M4P 2Y3, Canada (a division of Pearson Penguin Canada Inc.)
Penguin Books Ltd, 80 Strand, London WC2R 0RL, England
Penguin Ireland, 25 St Stephen's Green, Dublin 2, Ireland (a division of
Penguin Books Ltd)

Penguin Group (South Africa) (Pty) Ltd, 24 Sturdee Avenue, Rosebank,
Johannesburg 2196, South Africa

Penguin Books Ltd, Registered Offices: 80 Strand, London WC2R 0RL,
England

First published in Viking by Penguin Books India 2003
Published in Penguin Books 2009

Text copyright © Navtej Sarna 2003
Illustrations copyright © Penguin Books India 2003

The Book of
Nanak

NAVTEJ SARNA

ISBN 9780143066934

Typeset in Sabon by Manur Virtual Services, New Delhi
Printed at Saurabh Printers Pvt. Ltd, Noida

PENGUIN BOOKS

PENGUIN BOOKS
Published by the Penguin Group
Penguin Books India Pvt. Ltd, 11 Community Centre, Panchsheel Park,
New Delhi 110 017, India
Penguin Group (USA) Inc., 375 Hudson Street, New York, New York
10014, USA
Penguin Group (Canada), 90 Eglinton Avenue East, Suite 700, Toronto,
Ontario, M4P 2Y3, Canada (a division of Pearson Penguin Canada Inc.)
Penguin Books Ltd, 80 Strand, London WC2R 0RL, England
Penguin Ireland, 25 St Stephen's Green, Dublin 2, Ireland (a division of
Penguin Books Ltd)
Penguin Group (Australia), 250 Camberwell Road, Camberwell, Victoria
3124, Australia (a division of Pearson Australia Group Pty Ltd)
Penguin Group (NZ), 67 Apollo Drive, Albany, Rosedale, North Shore
0632, New Zealand (a division of Pearson New Zealand Ltd)
Penguin Group (South Africa) (Pty) Ltd, 24 Sturdee Avenue, Rosebank,
Johannesburg 2196, South Africa

Penguin Books Ltd, Registered Offices: 80 Strand, London WC2R 0RL,
England

First published in Viking by Penguin Books India 2003
Published in Penguin Books 2009

Text copyright © Navtej Sarna 2003
Illustrations copyright © Penguin Books India 2003

All rights reserved
10 9 8 7 6 5 4 3 2

ISBN 9780143066934

Typeset in Sabon by Mantra Virtual Services, New Delhi
Printed at Saurabh Printers Pvt. Ltd, Noida

Dedicated
to the beloved memory of my father
Mohinder Singh Sarna
and to the values that he cherished

Contents

Acknowledgements	*ix*
Introduction	1
The Stars Herald a Prophet	13
The Dark Times	19
The Early Years	29
The Divine Call at Sultanpur	41
And the Baba Went Along the Way . . .	51
As Far as the Land Stretched . . .	79
And Then He Climbed Sumer . . .	89
And Then the Baba Went to Mecca . . .	99
Kartarpur	109
The Teachings	121
The Hymns	129

Contents

Acknowledgements

This book would not have been possible but for the work done by several scholars, historians and poets on the life, times and teachings of Guru Nanak. To all of them I owe my gratitude, particularly to Sardar Harbans Singh, who treaded a careful path through the multitude of contradictions presented by the sources.

The translations of Guru Nanak's hymns by Sardar Manmohan Singh proved to be an invaluable base for my own attempt; the inconsistencies that exist are solely mine.

I would also like to thank Dr Jeevan S. Deol of Cambridge University for going through the manuscript and making very valuable suggestions.

Introduction

The five centuries that have elapsed since the time that Guru Nanak walked on this earth are but the blink of an eye in the history of men. Contemporaneous events are well known; men who lived at that time are well remembered. As I write these words, a glance outside the window takes me to the Lodhi tombs, still in good repair, where sultans from the Lodhi dynasty who ruled Delhi during Guru Nanak's lifetime lie buried. It was in Nanak's time that the first of the Mughals, Babar, invaded India several times, and finally, winning the first battle of Panipat, replaced Ibrahim Lodhi on the throne of Hindustan. His son Humayun, the white dome of whose tomb in Delhi shimmers in the hazy afternoon light, was battling to protect his fledgling empire when Nanak passed away. The Qutub Minar, whose once majestic domination of Delhi's skyline is now challenged by innumerable high-rise buildings, pre-dates Nanak's birth by more than two centuries.

Somewhat ironically, events that took place in other parts of the world during Guru Nanak's lifetime are even more current in our imagination. Columbus, in search of fabled India, stumbled upon the New World. Vasco da Gama found the route to India. Magellan completed the first voyage around the world. Corpus Christi College, that still stands at Oxford, was started, and Martin Luther took up the challenge of Reformation in Germany. We are not therefore dealing with one of the ancients, lost in the mist of time or remembered only through myths and hearsay. Guru Nanak, one of the greatest spiritual teachers mankind has known and the founder of India's youngest major religion, is young in human memory. His impact is recent, his message fresh.

What is lacking, and that is the reason that the above needed to be said, is precise historical detail regarding the life of Nanak, thus making it sound more distant than it actually is. There are no available records of that time, no exact itineraries of his incredible travels, no eyewitness accounts that would have brought home the immediacy of Nanak's world to us. For details of Guru Nanak's life we have to turn to sources which are not biographical in their approach: Nanak's own writings, Bhai Gurdas's first var or heroic ode, and the janamsakhis or anecdotal biographies, the earliest of which were written several decades after Nanak's death. Later writings on the life of Guru Nanak derive essentially from one or the other cycles of the janamsakhis and do not unearth new empirical data.

Guru Nanak's own writings are contained in nearly 1000 hymns in the Adi Granth, superb poetry set to divine music. These hymns however contain virtually no biographical details regarding places, dates and events connected with Nanak's life, with the possible exception of Babar's invasions. Nanak's message was predicated on the essential belief that he was only a messenger transmitting the divine word from the supreme reality to men. A detailed account of his life would have betrayed this belief.

A brief sketch of Guru Nanak's life was given by Bhai Gurdas, a nephew of the third Guru, Amar Das, in his first var. Stanzas twenty-three to forty-five of the var contain some biographical material on the life of Guru Nanak. This account, sketchy as it, is useful in that it comes from a source closely associated with the Gurus, fully aware of the message of Guru Nanak and its relevance in that age. The var was written about eighty years after Nanak died.

The genre of the janamsakhis is not one that lends itself easily to the historian's obsession with facts. Rather, the janamsakhis are popular forms of episodic narrative where names, places and dates are rarely mentioned. They do not follow any predictable chronology, and the authorship of the texts, with the exception of one, is unknown. They are written in Gurmukhi and the language used is Punjabi or Saddhukari. As is often the case with tales of spiritual teachers, the stories are imbued with drama and coloured by people's imagination and belief; as a result, myths, legends and miracles abound. Since there are clear contradictions among the different traditions of janamsakhis, there is no dearth of issues for pure academic inquiry—only a dearth of definitive sources.

All this however does not make the janamsakhis irrelevant. First, they are all we have. And second, a generous approach towards them, based on their intent and meaning, and armed with a spirit of reconciliation towards the obvious contradictions can help facilitate the reconstruction of the main events of Guru Nanak's life. It must always be kept in view that these janamsakhis were written not by historians but by believers. The origin of the janamsakhis would appear to be memories of Nanak as orally told and collectively recalled. To this is added, inevitably, piety, faith, reverence and contemporary belief of the writers themselves. The stories thus have a great value not simply as a record of events but as an interpretation of the doctrine. They are a graphic portrayal of the message rather than a mere description adhering strictly to the dictates of time and place.

It would be useful, before proceeding further, to take a brief look at the four traditions or cycles of janamsakhis. Most Sikh children, certainly of the last generation, have heard sakhis or stories at their grandmother's knee, in which Guru Nanak has not one but two companions, Bala and Mardana. Bala's name attaches to the most popular and influential of the traditions—Bhai Bala janamsakhi. The reason for the popularity of this set of janamsakhis is the claim, not taken seriously by most scholars, that it was dictated by

Bhai Bala in the presence of the second Guru, Angad Dev and forms an eyewitness account of Guru Nanak's life and travels. It is now believed that the Bhai Bala janamsakhi was grossly interpolated by the heretical sect of Hindalis.

The Puratan janamsakhi is the oldest, believed to be written about eighty years after the death of Guru Nanak. The first manuscript of the Puratan, known as the Vilayat-wali janamsakhi, was discovered 'partly destroyed by white ants' in 1872, though it had been brought to London in 1815 by Henry Thomas Colebrooke, a Sanskrit scholar and member of the council of the East India Company in Calcutta. The second manuscript was discovered by Bhai Gurmukh Singh of Oriental College, Lahore in Hafizabad and handed over to M.A. Macauliffe. This came to be known as the Hafizabad-wali janamsakhi. The two manuscripts were collated into a composite whole by the Sikh savant Bhai Vir Singh and published in 1926. A number of other manuscripts were found subsequently, including one dated 1640.

The third janamsakhi, discovered in 1940, is ascribed to Sodhi Meherban (1581–1640), grandson of the fourth Guru, Ram Das. His father Prithi Chand disputed the succession of Guru Arjan and fell away from the Sikh tradition. The shadow of these differences put into question the legitimacy of the Sodhi Meherban janamsakhi, but the recent discovery of an authentic manuscript has again revived interest in this janamsakhi which is now known for its author's obvious learning and his developed prose form.

The fourth collection is known as the Bhai Mani Singh janamsakhi. The prologue of this collection indicates its origins. When Bhai Mani Singh, a prominent Sikh at the time of Guru Gobind Singh, was requested to retell the janamsakhi of Guru Nanak and thereby remove the interpolations of the heretics, in particular the Minas (associated with the Meherban janamsakhi), he replied that he could not better Bhai Gurdas who had already written the janamsakhi in his first var. The Sikhs said they wanted an elaboration of the var and Bhai Mani Singh agreed to take up the job. The janamsakhi, as it stands today, combines an independent selection of sakhis with borrowings from the Bala tradition. In the epilogue it is mentioned that after the completion of the janamsakhi it was presented to Guru Gobind Singh for his signature. However, scholars have questioned the actual authorship by Bhai Mani Singh, arguing that his name was used more for the purpose of providing status and authenticity.

In view of the paucity of historical detail in the writings available on Guru Nanak's life, it is not possible to sift legend from fact completely. So this book follows the middle path of setting the abundant janamsakhi lore in as exact a historical framework as possible, and using it as a graphic, though at times exaggerated, portrayal of Guru Nanak's doctrine.

The aim here is not to establish incontrovertible historical detail, as that is hardly possible without the dramatic revelation of any new sources, but rather to understand the entire spiritual legacy of Nanak, the full significance of the message that he preached. The reconstruction of the main events of Guru Nanak's life is based on the broad chronology accepted by eminent Sikh scholars and is not necessarily confined to any particular janamsakhi cycle. Stories that sound too fantastic have not been included; at the same time, I have not made any attempt to water down or rationalize the mythical element of the original stories. The test lies in deciding whether a story, despite its mythical content, lies within the accepted legacy of Guru Nanak today, whether it highlights a particular aspect of his teachings. This choice is particularly difficult when it comes to describing Guru Nanak's travels, for the destinations and itineraries in the sources vary considerably. Bhai Gurdas has left a very reliable, if somewhat sketchy account; a more detailed and systematic account is to be found in the Meherban janamsakhi. Scholars have filled considerable gaps in the accounts by integrating them with the other janamsakhis and corroborating them with local traditions. With some rational

extrapolation of the material thus collated, fairly detailed
itineraries of Nanak's four great udasis, or missions,
have been drawn up. That is not to say that all
differences have been reconciled. Bhai Gurdas, for
instance, does not give details of any journey to the
south; the Meherban janamsakhi describes two journeys,
while the Puratan talks of four journeys, and this is more
widely accepted. While the visit to Mecca and Medina
is undisputed, the Meherban and Mani Singh
janamsakhis take the Guru as far afield as Palestine,
Turkey and Syria. In most accounts he has one
companion, Mardana; in some, he is accompanied by
Bala too. The chronology of the actual travels is also
not completely clear as the janamsakhis did not follow
any particular order, but concentrated more on the
events that took place and the messages they contained.
They are not therefore actual travel itineraries but rather
structures into which the various stories related to the
travels can be conveniently woven. Again the attempt,
in the present narrative, has been to follow the mainly
accepted stream of thought, tested against the logic of a
traveller in those times.

One last thought: the actual events of Guru Nanak's
lifetime and the debates about what did and what did
not happen, recede into the background when one
absorbs his message as contained in his own writings. A
reading of Guru Nanak's hymns is a deeply humbling

experience. We are immediately in the presence of a tremendous intellect, a deep philosopher, a phenomenal poet, a spiritual master. His was no ordinary life; this can be no ordinary story.

The Stars Herald a Prophet

The year was 1469 and the place was a small village called Rai Bhoe di Talwandi, about forty miles south-west of the city of Lahore. The village was surrounded by the dusty country of the Bar, or the edge of the jungle waste that lay in the Rachna doab, the tract of land between the Ravi and the Chenab. As far as the eye could see there was stunted bush vegetation and sand, broken only by patches of green around the village wells. This was a place of extreme weathers, frosty cold in winters and scorching hot in the long, dusty summers.

Not far from the village was one of the two main routes down which the invaders from Central Asia and Afghanistan thundered on their way to loot the riches of Hindustan and carry them away to their harsh homes in the arid mountains in the north-west. A victim of its location, Talwandi had been put to sword thirteen times, but each time it had come back to life from ruins.

To this village had come the family of Kalyan Chand, a Bedi Khatri by caste, from across the Ravi. Kalyan Chand or Mehta Kalu, as he was popularly known, became the revenue accountant for the Rai. It was to Mehta Kalu and his wife Tripta that Nanak was born, according to the Puratan janamsakhi, in 'Samvat 1526, month Baisakh, on the third day of the moonlit night, in the morning, three hours before dawn'.

The birth of Nanak was announced by the heavens

themselves. The humble room in which the birth took place suddenly became radiant. There was rejoicing among the wise in the celestial realms as well as on earth. Daulatan, the midwife, said that she had never seen a birth like that one—the first cry of the child was like the laughter of a wise, grown-up person joining a social gathering. The exultant father rushed to the house of Pandit Hardyal, the family priest, and requested him to make a horoscope for the child. Hardyal drew the constellations and made his calculations. Amazed by what he saw in the stars, Hardyal bowed to the newborn and pronounced that a great man had been born in Kalu's house who would be revered by Hindus and Muslims alike and whose name would be known on earth and in the heavens. Without doubt, Hardyal had seen in the stars that day that the prophet the age had been waiting for, had come.

That leaves one question unanswered: If Nanak was born in Baisakh, which corresponds to April, why is his birthday now celebrated on Kartik puranmasi, or the full-moon night that generally falls in November?

As late as 1815, during Maharaja Ranjit Singh's reign, the Gurupurab, or the Guru's birthday, was celebrated at Nankana Sahib in the month of Baisakh. The celebrations were later moved to the month of Kartik. The reason, according to some scholars, is that in Baisakh the peasants are busy with the harvest whereas in Kartik they are done with the autumn crop and more willing to congregate for the celebrations in better weather. A more convincing reason appears to be that it was on the full-moon night of Kartik that Nanak attained enlightenment after his bath in the Bein rivulet and came out of his trance with the revelation: 'There is no Hindu, no Mussalman.'

In any case, it is generally agreed that Guru Nanak died on Asauj Shudi 10 Samvat 1596 (22 September 1539) and that he lived for seventy years, five months and seven days. Working backwards, the date of birth is 15 April 1469. And there we must let it rest.

The Dark Times

The political events of the age, the social conditions and the religious landscape form an important context to Guru Nanak's life and teachings. When Nanak was born, the pillage of India at the hands of Timur in 1398 was still in living memory. For the half-century that had followed the visitation by the lame robber of Central Asia, Punjab had lived in spasmodic political turmoil. While the Sayyids ruled in Delhi, rebellion by three notorious leaders ensured that destruction was meted out regularly among the people of the land of the five rivers. Jasrat Khokar of Jhelum terrorized Punjab and reduced Lahore to a city of owls. He was followed in the pursuit of destruction by Sheikh Ali of Kabul and Folad Turkbacha of Bhatinda.

Some semblance of order was restored when Bahlol Lodhi took the throne of Delhi in 1451 and established his dynasty, destined to be the last of the Delhi sultanate. Guru Nanak was twenty when Sikander Lodhi sat on the throne. During his lifetime, Nanak saw the rule of Ibrahim Lodhi as well as his defeat at the hands of Babar after five invasions by the latter.

More immediate were the political conditions in Punjab. The western provinces of the Lodhi sultanate enjoyed relative political peace for the half-century following Nanak's birth. Tatar Khan Lodhi was the Governor of Lahore and Dipalpur till his death in 1485. In 1500, his son Daulat Khan Lodhi became the

Governor of Lahore and remained loyal to the Lodhis before turning against them and inviting Babar to invade Hindustan in 1523. Babar's invasions that had already begun in 1518 form the most dramatic political events of Nanak's lifetime and led to the defeat of the Lodhis in 1526. Babar died a decade or so before Nanak, and while Nanak lived the life of a householder at Kartarpur in his last years, Babar's son Humayun battled to strengthen the fledgling Mughal dynasty. At this stage, Punjab came under the sway of the Mughal governor, Mirza Kamran. A year after Guru Nanak's death, Kamran evacuated Lahore to Sher Shah and Humayun fled to Persia to seek assistance against the Suri.

Though for all practical purposes there was peace during the Lodhi years, these were not especially enlightened or happy times. The domination of the ruling race was complete, and Indian society, both Hindu as well as the non-privileged Muslim sections smarted under the whip of injustice, discrimination and exploitation. The rule of Sikander Lodhi (1488–1518) was particularly harsh on non-Muslims as the sultan was known to be overzealous and fanatical, with the non-Muslims having to pay the discriminatory 'jizya' tax to protect their life and property. The administrative and political machinery was largely the prerogative of the ruling race, the nobility being predominantly Afghan. Sunni Islam was the dominant religion of the ruling classes, though Shias and Ismailis also existed. The Qazis, Muftis and the Ulema, while trying to implement the Shariat, often reflected the bigoted approach of the rulers. However, the presence of Persian knowing non-Muslims in the lower rungs of the administrative and revenue set-up, particularly the class of muqaddams, was not unknown.

The provincial governors enjoyed a great degree of power in their regions. Punjab, it is said, did not suffer from instances of religious discrimination. That may well have been because of the disposition of men like Daulat Khan Lodhi, though that did not necessarily ensure a deliverance from the oppression of the ruling class or the administrative echelons. In fact Nanak's own words best describe the political conditions of the times:

> The dark times are like a knife,
> The Kings are butchers,
> Goodness has taken wings and flown;
> In the dark night of falsehood,
> The Moon of Truth,
> Is nowhere to be seen.

—Var Maja

He was openly critical of the rulers and their oppressive administrative machinery:

> The Kings behave like lions while their officials
> are dogs

—Var Malhar

And at another place:

Greed is the King, Sin his Minister,
Falsehood, master of the mint,
Lust is the trusted advisor—
Together they plan and plot

—Var Asa

Meanwhile, Hinduism had retreated defensively into orthodoxy and ritualism. Its responses to the times were severely hampered by the rigidity of the caste and the sub-caste systems. Weighed down by moribund traditions and completely at the mercy of the priestly class, Hindu society was a victim of dark superstition and defensive blind faith. The position of women was particularly backward and marked by practices of infanticide, child marriage and the boycott of widows from society. Hypocrisy and expediency provided convenient shelters from the harsh realities of the current day. These were propagated by those who had a vested interest in them—all manner of holy men who roamed the countryside and controlled every aspect of daily life. These men, in many coloured robes, ash smeared, carrying rosaries and pipes of hemp, their bodies naked in self-mortification, their consciousness clouded with charas and ganja, were the parasites of society. They encouraged gullibility and then fed on it. They terrorized the population, begging and threatening, telling fortunes, spouting curses, extracting money, food and shelter.

But there were also genuine ascetics, sanyasis and yogis. Prominent among the yogis of Punjab were the followers of Gorakhnath; the most accomplished of these were known as the ones with split ears, or the *kanphata* sect. Nanak was to take issue with such men several times and in his hymns there is ample criticism of the superficial nature of ritualistic practices.

> The Qazi tells untruths and eats filth
> The Brahmin kills and takes a holy bath
> The blind yogi knows not the true way
> All three make for mankind's ruin.
>
> —Raga Dhanasari

Given these conditions, a moral and spiritual regeneration was clearly called for. Nevertheless the situation was not completely lost. Hope lay in the Sufi movement in Islam and the Bhakti movement in Hinduism.

The Chisti and Suharawardy Sufi orders were the earliest to be established in India. The Sufi tradition underlined the mystical experience that arose out of a deep and personal love for God. The Sufis sought the ecstasy of union with God and suffered the anguish of separation. God was omnipresent and was everything.

The seeker needed to remember Him repeatedly. The Sufis preached tolerance and piety, equality of men and personal correctness. In the times of the Lodhis, the Sufis were well established in Punjab. Besides Lahore, Multan had become an important centre, particularly of the Suharawardy sheikhs. But the most important seat was at Pakpattan, that of Sheikh Fariduddin Ganj-i-Shakar. The Chisti sheikhs dominated Thanesar, Hansi, Narnaul and Panipat.

The Bhakti movement had come into its own in south India with Ramanuja giving a philosophical basis to the devotionalism of other earlier mystics. In north India, the tradition was propagated by Ramanand. He had several important followers—Ravidas, a shoemaker; Kabir, a Muslim weaver; Dhanna, a peasant and Sena, a barber. The Bhaktas inculcated the worship of one God, denounced priesthood and allegiance to ritualistic form, and broke through the barriers of caste. They preached belief in one God and urged an absorption in the absolute through expression of love.

Based on a passionately personal expression of love with the divine, both the movements taught the equality of men, control of worldly desires and avoidance of all forms of external piety. They had let loose a new freedom of thought and moral belief and provided the spiritual space needed to build a more flexible and resilient philosophical framework. They had also done something more—they had defined a narrow band of commonality between the two religions. However, in their purest form, Sufism and the Bhakti movement centred around the individual's private experience and did not aspire to become widespread religion for the common man. But the trends that they had set were to receive further impetus from Guru Nanak, who would bring to them an understanding purely his own and preach and inspire an integrated philosophy of life based not on ascetic renunciation or denial but on an affirmation of the reality of the world with the ultimate truth.

What the astrologer Hardyal saw in the stars on the morning of the birth of Nanak, would certainly come to pass. In the words of the poet Iqbal:

At last the voice of monotheism rose in the Punjab
An exalted being woke Hindustan from its slumber.

The Early Years

The son of Mehta Kalu and Tripta was a prodigious child. At the age of five, he amazed the villagers, Hindus and Muslims alike, by uttering words of spiritual wisdom. In fact, the Hindus among the villagers declared that a God had been born among them, while the Muslims celebrated the coming of a true follower of Allah.

When Nanak was seven years old, his father, keen that the child should acquire some basic education, decided to send him to Gopal, the priest-teacher who ran a small school for the village children. As recompense, Mehta Kalu took with him a tray of sweetmeats, rice, betelnut and a coin. But it soon became clear that Nanak was above ordinary learning and his mind would not be confined by the alphabet and the numbers. He amazed his teacher by writing, not just some letters of the alphabet but an entire poem on his patti or tablet. The poem or acrostic, known as 'Patti Likhi' ('Written on the Tablet'), is set in the Raga Asa and contained in the Adi Granth. Each stanza begins with one of the thirty-five letters of the Gurmukhi alphabet in serial order, and expounds eternal truths, like the omnipresence of divine reality and the transience of the material world. Nanak says the *maya* that surrounds this life can be cleared only through meditation on His name or simran. This bani or writings of the Guru shows not only Nanak's early understanding of the human condition

but also reveals his prodigious poetic talent that was to
mark all his later renditions.

> O foolish heart, why do you forget Him?
> When you render your account, O brother,
> Then alone will you be among the educated.
> —Raga Asa

Pandit Gopal was grateful for the presence of such
a gifted child in his class, but Nanak was not to stay
there for long. He soon left the school but composed
another song for Pandit Gopal, in which he revealed
the nature of true learning:

> Burn worldly love, pound it to ash and make
> thy ink,
> Turn thy intelligence into fine paper
> Make Lord's love thy pen, the mind thy scribe,
> Consult the Guru and write God's thoughts.
> Write the praises of God's name
> Write that He is without end, without limit
> O brother, learn to write such an account
> So where an account is asked for, your mark is true.
> —Raga Sri

Nanak began to show an increasing tendency to
withdraw into solitude and silence, and often he would

leave home and walk away into the fields and woods around the village to associate with wandering holy men. This worried his father, and a little later, when Nanak was nine years old, Kalu renewed his attempts to force Nanak to take lessons in traditional learning.

Rai Bular, the village landlord, assured Kalu that if Nanak learnt Persian, which was the language of the administration, he would be able to become the village accountant. So Nanak was sent to the Muslim maulvi of Talwandi to learn Persian. Once again the teacher was amazed at Nanak's quick grasp of the language. The maulvi proclaimed that a blessed child had come to him, one gifted by God himself with a vastly superior intelligence. After going to the maulvi for a few days, Nanak once again became silent and withdrawn and finally stopped going for his classes. He would lie despondently at home and paid little attention to the entreaties of his parents to get up and eat his food. In desperation, they called the maulvi home, hoping that Nanak would listen to him. The maulvi persuaded Nanak to get up for the sake of the God that he loved so much. Nanak then uttered a verse in Persian on man's transient existence in this world:

Know for certain in thy heart, this world perishes.

—Raga Tilang

The maulvi was astonished by the young child's perception and knowledge.

As was customary in Brahmin and Khatri families, Mehta Kalu arranged the yajnopavitam, or the ceremony of the sacred thread, for Nanak when he turned eleven. It was a momentous occasion and Kalu made elaborate arrangements, inviting a large number of friends and relatives to the occasion. Pandit Hardyal made all the customary arrangements for the sacred ceremony—the courtyard was washed and sanctified, incense lamps were lit and the floor decorated with holy signs. Amidst the chanting of holy mantras, Hardyal produced janeu, the sacred thread, made out of seven twisted and braided strings and long enough to go under one of the child's arms and stretch to the waist. As the priest proceeded to put the thread to the child's shoulder, Nanak inquired what he was doing. The priest explained that he was investing Nanak with the holy thread that would distinguish him as a member of the high castes. But Nanak waved him away. He said he saw no holiness in the thread. It would soil, wear out and break. Nanak then spoke to all who had gathered: Wearing a thread does not elevate a man; rather it is his actions and his commitment to the path of truthful living that distinguish him. His words are reflected in the Adi Granth:

From the cotton of Compassion, spin the thread of Contentment,

Give knots of Continence and twists of Truth;
This is the sacred thread for the soul—
If thou hast one such, O Brahman, then put it
on me.
It will not snap, nor soil; nor will it be burnt or
lost
Blessed is the man, O Nanak, who wears such
a thread around his neck.

—Raga Asa

The entire congregation was shocked by these bold words and the child's rejection of an ancient custom.

There were two people who recognized Nanak's extraordinary qualities very early in his childhood: his elder sister, Nanaki, and the Muslim village landlord, Rai Bular. While Nanaki doted all her life on her younger brother, Rai Bular's devotion was ignited by several events that he observed during Nanak's teenage years. The janamsakhis relate these events, using the vehicle of miracle.

Disturbed by Nanak's growing withdrawal and silence at home, and noting that he was much happier in the fields and forests, Kalu assigned him the responsibility of grazing the family buffaloes. Nanak would leave the buffaloes in the fields to graze while he meditated and felt at one with nature and with his own soul. He would also meet wandering ascetics and listen

to their discourses. On one such occasion, the buffaloes
trespassed into the abundant fields of a neighbour and
began to graze there. The owner of the field was livid
and insisted on taking Nanak to Rai Bular for justice.
The village chief called Mehta Kalu and told him to
recompense the aggrieved farmer. Meanwhile Rai
Bular's messengers had gone to check out the nature
and extent of the damage in the field. The messengers
came back with a surprising report. 'The owner is telling
lies,' they said. 'Not a blade of his crops has been
damaged.' The farmer was as surprised as everybody
else. He said that he had himself seen his crops being
destroyed by Nanak's buffaloes and only a divine miracle
could have restored the fields. The shrine of Kiara Sahib,
in Nankana Sahib, marks the field where this incident
is said to have taken place.

On another occasion, when the fields were ready
with their ripe crops, Rai Bular rode out with his servants
to measure the fields. When they were returning in the
hot summer afternoon, he saw that at a distance a boy
was sleeping under a tree while his cattle grazed in the
pasture. This by itself would not have attracted Rai
Bular's attention but he had noticed a strange
phenomenon. The shadows of all the other trees had
moved, following the dictates of the movement of the
sun. Only the shadow of the tree under which the boy
slept had not moved. It had stood still, as if its only

purpose was to provide shade to the sleeping boy. Rai Bular sent his servants to see who the boy was. They noticed that it was none other than Nanak, son of Kalu, and roused him. When Rai Bular saw Nanak, he got off his horse and embraced the boy, marvelling at the blessings of the Almighty on him. Later Rai Bular told Mehta Kalu: 'Your child is an exalted being. The village of Talwandi has been blessed by the presence of a great personality.'

The Bala janamsakhi tells the story of how, on another occasion, Rai Bular also witnessed a cobra spreading its hood over the face of the sleeping Nanak to protect it from the sharp rays of the sun at high noon. Rai Bular thus became one of the earliest followers of Guru Nanak. His belief and faith in Nanak's teachings grew from day to day. On several occasions, when Mehta Kalu would grow angry or dejected at the unworldly attitudes of his son, Rai Bular would console him: 'Nanak is a gem, Kalu, a man of God. Do not treat him like an ordinary person, do not rebuke him or berate him.'

Around this time, Nanak's marriage was arranged by his parents with Sulakhani, daughter of Mula, an inhabitant of Palihoke Randhawa village near Batala. In all probability, it was much later, when Nanak was nineteen and in Sultanpur that his wife came to live with him and bore him two sons—Sri Chand born in 1494 and Lakhmidas born in 1496. Sri Chand renounced worldly affairs and founded the ascetic order of Udasis, while Lakhmidas married and raised a family.

Nevertheless, the predicament of Nanak's parents was not easy to resolve. Out of their genuine concern for him, they wanted him to take up some occupation that a Khatri boy of his age was expected to be involved in—farm the land, keep shop or take up trading. However, the efforts of his father to convince him to involve himself in one of these activities bore no fruit. Nanak remained lost in meditation, happy in the company of wandering faqirs and sadhus. On one occasion this predeliction to distracted solitude took a serious turn. Nanak stopped stirring out of the house and ate or drank little for several days. The parents were deeply concerned and at a loss as to what to do. Some relatives urged them to call a physician to tend to the boy. Mehta Kalu went and got the village physician, Hardas. When Hardas tried to feel Nanak's pulse to diagnose the illness, Nanak stirred and told him that his suffering was not due to any ailment of the body:

> The physician has been called to cure me
> Holding my arm, he feels for the pulse
> Little does the simple physician know,
> The pain is in the soul.
>
> —Var Malhar

After discoursing with Nanak, the physician announced to the gathered relatives that they ought not to worry about the child's welfare. He was not an ordinary person but a great being. Much to the joy of his grateful parents, Nanak eventually regained his appetite and his health.

Still meaning to arouse his interest in the affairs of the world, Kalu once gave Nanak twenty silver coins. He told him to go and invest them in a profitable manner by purchasing goods such as salt and turmeric from the nearby market town of Chuharkana and then selling them at a profit. Bala, a Sandhu Jat, was assigned to accompany Nanak and to assist him. 'Make a truly good bargain,' his father said, as he watched his son and Bala go on their way.

Their way lay through a forest where they came upon a group of sadhus, performing penance of all kinds. Their chief told Nanak that they were a group of *nirbani* sadhus, who wore no clothes and ate only when the Almighty sent food. In the event, Nanak discovered that they had not eaten for several days. Nanak knew that he had found the best bargain that he could ever hope to strike. He reached the market town, and ignoring Bala's protests, spent all the money that his father had given him on buying provisions—wheat, sugar, ghee—for the sadhus. On returning home, Bala recounted the events to Mehta Kalu, and fearing his ire, clarified that

Nanak paid no heed to his advice. Nanak, anticipating his father's angry reaction, did not go home but sat under a tree outside the village. When Kalu found him and began to berate him for wasting the money, it was once again Nanaki and Rai Bular who prevailed upon Mehta Kalu to treat Nanak as distinct from the ordinary.

But Nanaki was soon to leave Talwandi. One day Jairam, a Khatri revenue official of Sultanpur, in the employ of the governor of Lahore, Nawab Daulat Khan Lodhi, came to Talwandi to assess the revenue demand of the village. Noting the presence of a number of good Khatri families in the village, Jairam sought Rai Bular's advice in the matter of finding a bride for himself. Rai Bular suggested that Jairam seek the hand of Mehta Kalu's daughter Nanaki. Thus the thirteen-year-old Nanaki was married to Jairam and left her parents and her beloved younger brother to accompany her husband to Sultanpur. Nanak's deep attachment to his sister and the mutual respect in which he and Jairam held each other were to provide a fitting cause for him to move to Sultanpur some years later.

The Divine Call at Sultanpur

The prosperous town of Sultanpur lay at the confluence of the Sutlej and Beas rivers. It was built by Daulat Khan Lodhi, who ruled there as the governor of Jallandhar doab. In all probability it was built on the site of the old Tamasvana Buddhist monastery, which finds mention in the writings of the great traveller, Hieun Tsang.

While Mehta Kalu and other family members became despondent with the lack of interest that Nanak showed in worldly affairs, his brother-in-law, Jairam, had formed a very postive impression of him. He and Rai Bular felt that Nanak was a saint and was misunderstood by his father. After Nanaki had settled with Jairam in Sultanpur, Jairam wrote a letter to Mehta Kalu, inviting Nanak to come and stay with them in Sultanpur, expressing his hope that he could find employment for Nanak. Though it was not customary for a younger brother to go and stay at the house of his married elder sister, Kalu consulted Rai Bular and agreed to let Nanak go, thinking that the change would prove to be good for him. So Nanak set out for Sultanpur, blessed by his parents and seen off by childhood friends and companions. Among the companions that he left behind was Mardana, the Muslim dum or musician, who used to accompany him on a reed rabab when he sang his hymns in Talwandi. Mardana was to eventually join Nanak in Sultanpur and accompany him on his extensive travels.

The journey from Talwandi to Sultanpur took five days. On the way Nanak crossed the Ravi near Lahore and the Beas near Goindwal. When he finally arrived in Sultanpur, Nanaki's joy knew no bounds. In a few days, Jairam fixed an audience for Nanak with the governor, Daulat Khan Lodhi. The governor was immensely impressed with Nanak's appearance and demeanour and offered to appoint him his storekeeper. This was an important charge those days as the taxes were collected in kind and the salaries were at least partly paid out in grains and provisions. Nanak began to apply himself fully to his job, spending his days hard at work at the modikhana or the comissariat. From all accounts, Daulat Khan was very pleased with his work. At one stage, some detractors spread the canard that Nanak was giving away food grain from the official store. But when an investigation took place, the balance was found to be in favour of the storekeeper. While he worked he remained deeply engrossed in the meditation of the supreme being. Once, when he was weighing the rations, he reached the figure thirteen, or tera in Punjabi. He kept repeating tera, tera, tera because it also meant 'Thine, Thine, Thine, all is Thine'.

Thus, Nanak's spiritual quest continued unabated. He had formed a group of companions with whom he prayed and meditated in the evenings. Mardana was sent by Mehta Kalu from Talwandi to check how Nanak was doing. When he arrived in Sultanpur, he decided to stay there as Guru Nanak's companion.

Early morning, before the crack of dawn, Nanak would go and bathe in the Bein river that flowed to the north-west of the town. There he would remain absorbed in the contemplation of the Almighty and remembrance of the divine name. One day he did not return home after his morning bath; later his clothes were found on the bank of the river, leading people to think that he had been taken by the current. Daulat Khan himself visited the river bank, and when the fishermen's nets that had been flung into the water to retrieve the body turned up empty, he too lamented the loss of his 'good minister'.

After three days, to the utter amazement of all, Nanak reappeared. The janamsakhis explain the disappearance as a mystical communion with the Almighty. In the court of God, His grace was bestowed upon him as Nanak was given the cup of the truthful name and a robe of honour. It is during this experience, say the janamsakhis, that Nanak uttered the lines which form the essence of his message, the first stanza of the Japji, which represents the essence of Guru Nanak's teachings and is the authentic revelation of supreme reality:

There is but one God, true is His Name,
The Creator, fearless, without rancour,
Timeless, unborn, self-existent
By God's grace he is known
Meditate on Him
He was true
In the beginning, in the primal time,
O Nanak, true He is and will be hereafter.

On his reappearance, Nanak was silent, leading the townspeople to believe that he had been taken over by an evil spirit. When he finally spoke, his words surprised everyone: 'There is no Hindu and there is no Mussalman.'

To him this was a simple statement of the essential equality of all human beings, irrespective of creed. But in a society segregated on the basis of religion, a society in which creed and caste were the basis of everything, such a statement was heresy. News of Nanak's astounding utterance reached the Qazi of Sultanpur. The Qazi strode in anger to Daulat Khan Lodhi and urged him to summon Nanak to his court. Daulat Khan was however inclined to take a more generous view and to dismiss the comment as one which could be uttered by a faqir. But the Qazi was insistent. Finally Daulat Khan sent his messengers to bring Nanak before him. When Nanak appeared in court, it was time for the afternoon namaz and he accompanied the nawab and the Qazi to the mosque. There he stood by as the Qazi knelt to conduct the prayers. This further angered the Qazi who complained again to the nawab that though Nanak preached that there was no difference between Hindus and Muslims, he refused to kneel in prayer with the Muslims.

'Whose prayer do I join?' asked Nanak. 'The Qazi is only repeating empty words. His mind is on his new born foal running loose in his yard. He is worried that the foal may fall into the well. And as for you, respected governor, you were thinking of purchasing horses in Kabul.' Both the Qazi and the governor admitted that their minds had indeed not been in the prayer. In the Granth Sahib, Nanak says:

> It is not easy to be called a Musalman:
> If one be truly so, let him be so known.
> First, he should take to heart his faith
> And rid himself of all pride
> Become a true disciple of the Prophet
> And overcome the illusion of life and death;
> He should accept the will of God Supreme,
> Believe in the Creator, efface his ego
> When he is merciful to all living beings, O Nanak,
> Then will he be called a Musalman.
>
> —Var Majh

On hearing these words, the nawab fell at Nanak's feet. All questions had been answered and all doubts had been set at rest. Nanak, to fulfil his role as the divine messenger, was now ready to leave Sultanpur to spread the divine word in all directions. Daulat Khan begged Nanak not to leave Sultanpur, placing at his disposal his dominion and authority, but Nanak was beyond temptations. The path that he had to follow lay clearly before him:

Were there to be palaces of pearls, studded with gems,
Plastered with musk, saffron and sandal
And their very sight should fill the heart with joy;
May I not even then forget Thy thoughts,
And neglect to meditate on Thy Name!

—Raga Sri

Bhai Gurdas sums up Guru Nanak's Sultanpur experience thus:

First he found the door to Heaven
And then worked hard to gain His Grace
Eating what he found, sleeping where he could,
He meditated deeply and attuned with the Divine

And was awarded the Divine Name and Humility
He saw only suffering in all directions
Without God, only darkness everywhere
He set out then to spread the word.

—Var I, 24

It was in the year 1496 that the twenty-seven-year-old Nanak bid goodbye to Sultanpur. To his beloved sister Nanaki, he gave a special blessing—he would visit her whenever she wished it deep in her heart.

Today several shrines mark Guru Nanak's stay in Sultanpur—Gurdwara Hatti Sahib used to be Nanak's store; Kothri Sahib is the room where he used to settle the account with the nawab; Guru Ka Bagh was the residence of Jairam and Nanaki; Sant Ghat commemorates the place of Nanak's immersion in the Bein rivulet.

And the Baba Went Along the Way . . .

Guru Nanak spent as many as twenty-three years on the road, carrying out the mission that he was charged with—to spread the ultimate truth and to put mankind on the path to salvation. In the days when there were no fast or sophisticated means of travel, Nanak visited Assam in the east, present-day Sri Lanka in the south, Mount Kailash in the north and Mecca in the west. His mission took him to snowy heights and across burning deserts, through little villages and mighty capitals, among the ordinary as well as the learned, to fairs and festivals, to temples, mosques and Sufi *khanaqahs*. In the poetic vision of Bhai Gurdas: 'The Baba traversed the nine regions of the earth, as far as the land stretched.' Gurdwaras and shrines mark Nanak's travels to far-flung places; local legends and evidence such as well-preserved impressions of Nanak's wooden sandals further establish the fact that Nanak travelled extensively.

Nanak was accompanied by Mardana on his travels, who carried his rabab. He dressed in strange clothes that could not be identified with any sect and symbolized the universality of his message. He wore the long, loose shirt of a Muslim dervish but in the brownish-red colour of the Hindu sanyasi. Around his waist he wore a white kafni or cloth belt like a faqir. A flat, short turban partly covered a Qalandar's cap on his head in the manner of Sufi wanderers. On his feet, he wore wooden sandals, each of a different design and colour. Sometimes, it is said, he wore a necklace of bones around his neck.

The first udasi or spiritual mission, of Guru Nanak, which was to take him to the east, began with a series of short trips within Punjab. Soon after Nanak and Mardana started the journey from Sultanpur Mardana complained of hunger, as he was to do on several occasions in the years to come. Guru Nanak pointed out to him the village of Uppal Khatris and told him that if he went there, all his desires would be met. When Mardana reached the village, he was not only fed to his heart's content but was also given a bundle of clothes and money. When he brought the bundle back with him, Guru Nanak laughed. He advised Mardana to throw away the bundle and told him not to accept such encumbrances on their journey.

As they crossed the Beas, Nanak came across a grove of trees that enclosed a natural lake. Charmed by the spot, he meditated under a berry tree. The tree still stands on the north embankment of the lake at the Golden Temple in Amritsar. From there Nanak went on to Lahore for a brief visit and then came back to the village of Talwandi. His ageing parents and Rai Bular, his great admirer, were delighted to see him. It also gave Mardana a chance to spend time with his friends and family.

From Talwandi, Nanak and Mardana proceeded to the north-west for about sixty miles until they came upon the town of Saidpur Sandiali. This town was later to be sacked by Babar and renamed Eminabad, after the name of a waterman's wife who gave him parched gram to eat.

On reaching Saidpur, Nanak proceeded straight to the house of Lalo, a humble carpenter, avoiding the rich houses of the city. Mardana watched, fascinated, as Nanak talked to the poor hard-working carpenter in a gentle voice and shared his coarse bread as if it were a sumptuous dish of food. Lalo was soon captivated by the sweet and serene message of the Guru. He requested the Guru to stay a little longer in his humble dwelling. Since the association was against popular custom the word soon spread that a holy man who went by the name of Nanak and who was born in a Khatri family in nearby Talwandi was staying with a low-caste carpenter. Meanwhile Malik Bhago, a rich Hindu diwan of the Muslim local chief of Saidpur, threw a feast in which he invited all the sadhus and faqirs in the vicinity. On the day of the feast, a veritable crowd gathered around the rich man's house. However, it was reported to him that the Khatri faqir who was staying with the low-caste carpenter had chosen not to attend the feast. Malik Bhago was curious and angry. Messengers were sent immediately to bring Nanak to the feast. When Guru Nanak reached the festivities, Malik Bhago asked him the reason for not attending the feast. 'Do you find the food at the house of your casteless host better than mine?' he asked.

According to the Bala janamsakhi, as Nanak was asked to savour rich dishes of Malik Bhago's feast, he asked that some food be brought from Lalo's house too. He then held Lalo's coarse bread in his right hand and Malik Bhago's delicacies in his left. When he squeezed both his hands, milk dropped out of the coarse bread and blood from the delicacies. Nanak's message to the amazed onlookers was clear. Blessed is the simple bread earned by hard work and shared with one's neighbour and cursed the wealth collected through the imposition of suffering on others.

Lalo's hut became the meeting place of Nanak's disciples, both Hindus and Muslims. There they gathered to sing hymns in the praise of the Almighty and to meditate on the true omnipresent creator. Guru Nanak was to visit Lalo several times in the years to come. It is not the chronology of his visits to Saidpur, but rather the association with Lalo and the observations contained in the poetry linked to Lalo that are important.

Guru Nanak's visit to the town of Tulamba in south-west Punjab is famous for the story of the transformation of Sajjan, the thug. Besides the highway along which wayfarers passed lived Sheikh Sajjan, apparently a pious man who gave food and shelter to weary travellers, notwithstanding their creed or religion. However, at night when they slept, the pious man would turn into what he actually was—a highway bandit and murderer. He would kill the unsuspecting guests and take away their goods and money, and return to his apparent God-fearing ways in the morning. As he courteously received Guru Nanak, he was convinced that a man of Nanak's radiance must be wealthy and he could hardly wait for the guest to retire. However, when night fell and he came to the Guru's door, he found that the Guru was singing hymns of devotion and the accompanying sweet sounds of Mardana's rabab filled the night. Sajjan was captivated. The music and the words seemed to touch some inner chord deep within his heart. He felt an inner enlightenment and peace that he had never experienced before. He fell at Guru Nanak's feet, confessed his sins and asked for forgiveness. Thereafter, he gave away in charity all his ill-gotten property and converted his house into a true dharamsala. The tomb of Sajjan and a ruined mound that bears his name is said to exist in the present-day town of Makhdumpur in Pakistan.

Moving towards Delhi, Nanak reached the ancient town of Kurukshetra, also known as the navel of the earth and the site of the great battle between the Kauravas and the Pandavas in the Mahabharata. Here a great fair was being held to mark the solar eclipse. Guru Nanak decided to challenge the extreme orthodox views that had turned vegetarianism into a rigid fetish by cooking the meat of a deer that had been brought by a disciple. This angered the Brahmins who protested that the cooking of meat on such an auspicious day was an act of deliberate profanity. The Guru responded that man was deeply attached to flesh; he was born of flesh and was flesh himself, so why be averse to it? Who was the sinner—the one who ate flesh or the one who excluded it from his food?

> . . . Those who abjure meat
> And sit holding their noses
> Eat men at night;
> They make a show of hypocrisy for others
> But have no true knowledge of God.

> . . . From flesh are born
> Women, men, kings, emperors,
> If you see them going to Hell,
> Then take thee not their charity
> Strange justice—the giver goes to Hell
> And the receiver to Heaven!
> O Pandit, you understand not yet preach,
> You indeed are wise!
>
> —Var Malhar

Nanak then passed through Panipat where he met the successor of the renowned Sufi saint Sheikh Sharaf,

also known as Abu Ali Qalandar. In the discourse that
followed, the sheikh who was then in charge of the centre
queried Nanak about his manner of dress, religious
beliefs and so on. Extremely pleased with the answers
he received, the Sufi sheikh introduced Nanak to his
followers as: 'What credentials do we need of one who
has witnessed God? Just to look upon him is enough.'

Finally Guru Nanak, accompanied by Mardana,
entered Delhi and was welcomed by both Hindu and
Muslim devotees. He stayed in the dwelling of a pious
Muslim faqir named Majnu on the banks of the Yamuna.
He initiated Majnu in the mysteries of the supreme lord
and held discourses there for several days for both
Muslim and Hindu sects. A massive gurdwara, Majnu
Ka Tila marks the spot today. The Puratan janamsakhi
also records that Nanak spent a night in Delhi at the
camp of the sultan's *mahouts*. That night one of the
elephants died, leading to lamentations all around, as
the death would deprive the mahout of his source of
livelihood. The Guru forbade the mahouts from crying
and urged them instead to pray to God. When they did,
it is said that the elephant came back to life. The next
day, the sultan rode the same elephant and came to see
Nanak. The sultan then bade the Guru to kill and revive
the elephant again but Nanak refused, saying that life
and death were in the hands of God.

Returning from Delhi, Guru Nanak and Mardana

saw a sheikh named Wazid being carried in the comfort of a palanquin by his servants. When the palanquin was laid down in the shade of a tree, a comfortable bed was made out for the sheikh. As the sheikh sprawled on the bed, his servants proceeded to massage and fan him. The spectacle prompted Mardana to ask the Guru, 'Tell me, Master, is there one God who made this man who gets tired in the comfort of his palanquin and another who made those poor men who run on naked feet carrying him and even now massage and press his legs?'

'Strange are the ways of God,' Nanak said. 'There may be impoverishment in abundance while poverty itself may be abundant. Only his grace gives understanding.'

Nestling in the foothills of the Garhwal Himalayas, Hardwar was, as it still is, an important centre of Hindu pilgrimage. The chanting of hymns in the town's myriad temples, the sound of conch shells and the crowds of holy men on the banks of the Ganga distinguished the town. Nanak and Mardana went to the crowded banks of the Ganga and watched the pilgrims as they pushed their way to the river and bathed themselves in the holy waters. For many of them it was the end of a long journey; they had travelled from distant towns and villages to wash away their sins and pray to God for forgiveness. Nanak observed that the pilgrims were cupping water in their hands and tossing it towards the rising sun in the east. Nanak himself entered the water and, with his back to the sun, started throwing water towards the west. The pilgrims thought that he was a crazy man and asked him, 'What manner of man are you? Muslim or Hindu? If you are a Muslim, what are you doing here? If you are a Hindu, why are you throwing water away from the sun?'

'Why are you throwing water towards the sun?' asked Nanak, while continuing to throw water towards the west.

'It will bring peace to the spirits of our ancestors.'

The Guru again resumed throwing water towards the west. The pilgrims persisted with their questions. Finally, the Guru replied, 'I have left my field near my home in the west. There is no one to irrigate it and the rain water does not stay. I am throwing water to sprinkle my crops.' The pilgrims were incredulous. 'How can your water reach your field from here, so many miles away?' Nanak replied that if their water could reach their ancestors in heaven, then his field was, comparatively speaking, only a stone's throw away. His message was simple—merit lay in the true love of God, not in empty ritual.

As they bathed and prayed, the pilgrims normally spent several days in Hardwar. In the evenings, they would sit in groups and cook their food. Nanak noticed that they would draw circles on the ground, sprinkle

them with water and cook food only within the circle.
These circles were meant to keep out the shadow of any
low-caste person who may happen to pass by. Nanak
spoke to the pilgrims and told them that the real pariahs
were the evil elements that dwelt in one's own heart—
evil thoughts, heartlessness, slander of others—and man
had to guard himself against them. What good would
the drawing of lines in the ground do when such pariahs
were seated within one's own self?

> Truth, Self-discipline, right action
> Are the lines to draw
> Contemplation of His Name
> Is the holy bath
>
> —Raga Sri

Leaving behind the plains and foothills of Uttar
Pradesh, Nanak followed the ancient and difficult
pilgrim routes into the mountains of Garhwal, the land
of sacred rivers and revered mountain peaks of gods
and goddesses. Guru Nanak walked towards Joshimath,
passing through the great Hindu pilgrimage centres at
Kedarnath and Badrinath. From Joshimath, he probably
walked across the Antra and Lepu La passes and then
along the Kali river towards Almora. Thereafter, and
here again the sources vary as to when, he passed
through several well-known places, including

Gorakhmata, Ayodhya, Varanasi and Prayag. Local traditions and historical gurdwaras have preserved the memories of his visits and the events that took place.

Thirty odd miles east of Haldwani is Gurdwara Retha Sahib. This shrine marks the place where Mardana once again complained to Guru Nanak that he was hungry. To assuage his hunger, the Guru pointed to a tree of bitter soapnuts. When Mardana shook a branch and put one of the nuts in his mouth, he found that it was not bitter but sweet. The tree at Retha Sahib still partially bears sweet nuts which pilgrims from far and wide take away as prasad.

At a distance of another thirty miles in the Terai region was a forest abode of Nath yogis, followers of Gorakh. This cult practised tantric rituals and it was not usual for outsiders to venture into their forest retreat. Guru Nanak and Mardana proceeded towards their camp and sat under a dried-up tree. Mardana walked up to one of the yogis to ask for a light with the help of which they could build a fire in the cold winter night. The yogi turned him away angrily. But when the tree under which Nanak had camped began to sprout new leaves, the yogis were impressed and entered into a discourse with the visitor. After challenging him with their various miracles and listening to his responses, they invited Nanak to join their faith. His answer is contained in the Adi Granth:

Religion lies not in the yogi's patched garment,
Nor in his staff
Nor in covering the body with ashes.
Religion lies not in wearing large rings
From split ears
Nor in shaving the head nor in the blowing of
the conch
To live pure amid temptations of the world
Is to understand religion.

—Raga Suhi

The yogis hailed Nanak as an exalted one.
Gorakhmata later changed its name to Nanakmata and
it lies just fifteen miles away from the present-day town
of Pilibhit. In that area one can find followers of Nanak,
known as Nanakpanthis.

The Puratan janamsakhi tells of a shopkeeper who
became a follower of Guru Nanak during the latter's
travels and came every day to serve the Guru. One day,
another shopkeeper accompanied him out of curiosity
to see Nanak. But on the way he was captivated by the
charms of a woman. Subsequently, they would leave
their village together, one to serve the Guru and the
other to visit his mistress. One day they wanted to test
the result of their actions and decided to meet at the end
of the day at an appointed place. The first man as usual
visited Guru Nanak, but as soon as he left the Guru's

presence, his toe was pierced by a thorn. He went to the meeting place with a bandage on his toe and his slipper in his hand. The other man did not find his mistress at home that day and came to the appointed place ahead of time. As he was sitting there he scratched the ground with a stick. The stick hit a gold mohur, and on digging further, the man unearthed a jar of charcoal. When they met up, they both decided to go back to Guru Nanak to be enlightened on the ways of God—the virtuous man had been injured by a thorn but the sinner had found a gold mohur. Nanak told them that the ways of God were strange. It could well be that the virtuous acts of the first man had changed what could have been an impaling stake into a mere thorn while the other's sins had changed what could have been a jar of gold mohurs into a single mohur and turned the rest to charcoal.

> Man's conduct is the paper
> On which, the mind's quill
> Records both good and evil
> As our deeds dictate, we live,
> But God's Grace knows no end.

—Raga Maru

During their journey, Guru Nanak and Mardana were once accosted on the road by a group of thugs, who were deceived by the glow on Nanak's face into believing that he must be a man of means. Nanak pointed out to them the smoke of a funeral pyre and told them to first go and get fire from the pyre so that they could cremate him and Mardana after killing them. The Puratan janamsakhi says that when the thugs went to the pyre, they saw a tussle for the dead man between the angels and the messengers of Yam, the god of death. The angels explained that the dead man had been a big sinner and his soul was not meant for salvation, but the Guru's glance at the smoke from his pyre had saved his soul. The thugs immediately returned to Guru Nanak and expressing their deep repentance, sought his forgiveness. Guru Nanak advised them to give up their evil ways, take to agriculture and make an honest living.

Ayodhya, the birthplace of Lord Ram, lay across the Ghaggra river. Guru Nanak preached his message of love and tolerance there at the festival marking the return of Ram from his fourteen-year exile in the forests. He told the Bairagi sadhus how religion did not necessarily lie in renunciation but could be obtained while being part of the world. Right conduct, love, service and the grace of God was all that was required. At Prayag, where the Ganga meets the Yamuna in the *sangam*, he enthralled pilgrims and devotees with his sweet songs. When a priest urged him to bathe in the holy waters, Nanak asked how the bathing of the body would cleanse the impurities of the heart.

The road to Varanasi from Prayag lay along the left bank of the Ganga. In Varanasi, the birthplace of Kabir, Nanak saw groups of Brahmins and acolytes, Vaishnavite sadhus and bare-bodied ascetics. This was the heart of rigid orthodoxy. With penance and prayer all over the place, Nanak felt it necessary to communicate his message of enlightened humanism here.

A leading pandit by the name of Chatur Das accosted him, 'What faith do you follow? You do not carry the *saligram* and you wear no necklace of tulsi leaves.' Nanak replied:

> O Brahmin,
> You worship and propitiate the stone god
> And deem it a good act
> To wear a rosary of sweet basil
> Why irrigate land that is waste?
> Why plaster a weak, falling wall?
>
> . . . Build a raft of the Lord's name
> And pray He shall ferry you across.
>
> —Raga Basant Hindol

Chatur Das, after a lengthy discussion, realized the wisdom of what Guru Nanak had said and became his disciple. He was joined by others who were also impressed by the message of Nanak. According to the

Puratan janamsakhi, it was here at Varanasi that Nanak enunciated the fifty-four stanzas of his composition *Dakhni Onkar*.

> Performing rituals does not release one
> Without virtue one goes to the city of death
> He gains neither this world, nor the one beyond
> The sinner in the end regrets
> He possesses neither knowledge, nor concentration,
> Nor any faith, nor meditation
> Without the Name he cannot be fearless
> Nor understand the evil of ego
> I am tired; how do I reach
> The Unfathomable, the Endless!
> I do not have loved friends
> To whom I may appeal for help
> Nanak, if I utter my beloved's name
> The Uniter shall Unite me with Himself
> If I love Him boundlessly
> The one who separates shall unite.
> —Ramkali Dakhni Onkar, 37

Guru Nanak and Mardana were now headed towards the next major centre of pilgrimage, important to both Hindus and Buddhists: Gaya, in Bihar. There, on the bank of the Phalgu river, the local priests supervised large-scale ceremonies that consisted of offering funeral barley cakes to departed ancestors and lighting lamps that would light up the paths of the departed spirits in the heavens above. The priests tried their best to make Nanak join these ceremonies but the Guru refused, saying that only man's deeds could help him in the next world.

> The Lord is my barley roll and leaf platter
> The Creator's true name is my obsequy.
> —Raga Asa

Impressed by Nanak's teachings, the chief priest of Bodhgaya, Dev Gir, became a disciple of Nanak and began to lead the local congregation.

From Gaya a path led to the town of Hajipur, on the northern bank of the Ganga, at its confluence with the Gandak. Close to Hajipur were the ruins of ancient Pataliputra, where the later city of Patna, the birthplace of the tenth Guru, Gobind Singh was to rise. An old gurdwara marks Nanak's visit to Hajipur. Here too Mardana complained of hunger. The Guru gave him a stone that he had picked up on the way and told Mardana to go into the town and buy some food with it. Mardana went from shop to shop and was turned away empty-handed until he came to the shop of Salis Rai, a scholar. Salis Rai looked at the stone carefully and immediately wanted to meet the owner of such a priceless jewel. Accompanied by his servant Adhrakka, he followed Mardana to Nanak and, recognizing a great soul, became the Guru's true disciple. His descendant, Fateh Chand Maini, was to become a favourite disciple of Guru Gobind Singh.

Further to the east, across Bengal, lay the fabled land of Kauru or Kamrup, known for its women sorceresses who practised the awe-inspiring cults of magic and tantra. The story goes that Mardana, on reaching this land, begged the Guru to let him go in search of food. The Guru told him to go if he must but also warned him that he should be careful for here the women were steeped in the secrets of witchcraft. Despite the warning, Mardana was captivated by an enchantress who beckoned him to come to her house. As he entered her doorway, she cast a spell on him and turned him into a ram. When the Guru came and saw the ram tied in the house, he demanded that Mardana be returned to him. The enchantress then tried her spell on Nanak. When she could make no headway, she enlisted the help of other women magicians, described in some versions as women riding a tree, or mounted on the moon or accompanied by a tiger. They too failed to have any impact on Nanak and he released Mardana from the spell by casting one look at him. Then arrived the queen of the sorceresses, Nur Shah, and she tried all her tricks, including the most attractive dances and songs to make Nanak a captive. Her attendants brought pearls and diamonds, gold and silver, and laid them at his feet. Guru Nanak rejected all the gifts and sang of the qualities of a virtuous woman. Finally, Nur Shah and her attendants submitted to Guru Nanak and sought the path to salvation. Guru Nanak told them to renounce the practice of magic and turn their energies to domestic duties. This story is evocative of the Guru's message against tantra, black magic and other obscurantist practices.

Several places in modern-day Assam, or Asa desh as it is known in the janamsakhis, also bear the marks of Guru Nanak's visits and discourses. The most famous of these places is Dhubri, in Goalpara district, where the Guru is said to have met Shankardev, the Vaishnavite reformer. In the year 1667, the ninth Sikh Guru, Tegh Bahadur followed in Nanak's footsteps and established a shrine at Dhubri in memory of Guru Nanak's visit.

Guru Nanak's travels through Assam led him to Guwahati and then on to Manipur, identified in the sakhis as the country of Bisiar. Moving in the south-western direction, the Guru moved to Shillong, Sylhet, Chittagong and Dhaka. In Dhaka, as in many other places, there is a shrine called Charan Paduka (wooden sandals from holy feet) that is part of the strong local tradition supporting the visit of the Guru. Passing through Calcutta and Cuttack, the Guru is then said to have reached Puri in Orissa, the site of the famous temple of Jagannath.

Jagannath temple is known for its annual procession when the idol is mounted on a huge chariot and the multitudes that gather vie with each other for the privilege of pulling the chariot. It is an inexorable sea of humanity that moves with the idol, a phenomenon that gave the word 'juggernaut' to the English language. When Guru Nanak and Mardana camped near the temple, their hymns and music attracted several devotees on their way to the temple, annoying the temple priests. One day the chief priest, Krishanlal, came to Nanak and invited him to join the aarti, or the evening prayer, in the temple, and Guru Nanak readily accompanied him.

It was a beautiful ceremony, conducted at dusk. The priests placed earthen lamps filled with ghee on a bejewelled salver decorated with flower petals and sweet incense. They lit the wicks and swung the salver, pendulum-like, in front of the image while the congregation sang hymns, blew conches and tolled the bells that hung from the ceiling. Nanak sat unmoved through the ceremony, and when the priests expressed their anger at this, he responded with a song, that is now included in the Granth Sahib. This song describes a celestial aarti in which the sky, the sun, the moon, the

stars, the wind, the forests and the unstruck music pay
obeisance to the great creator. This, according to Nanak,
was the only aarti that could be offered to God.

> The sky the salver, the sun and moon the lamps,
> The stars studding the heavens are the pearls
> The fragrance of sandal is the incense
> Fanned by the winds, all for Thee
> The great forests are the flowers.
> What a beautiful aarti is being performed
> For you, O Destroyer of fear.
>
> —Raga Dhanasari

More than three and a half centuries later,
Debendranath Tagore, the father of Rabindranath,
visited the Golden Temple and listened to this aarti being
sung after the evening prayers. He was so moved by it
that he decided to learn Gurmukhi to read the Adi
Granth in the original. Later he included the entire song
in the Bangla script in his autobiography. The visit to
Jagannath Puri is also important for the meeting between
Nanak and the Bengal reformer Chaitanya
Mahaprabhu. It is on record that they talked to each
other and sang hymns together.

According to the Puratan tradition, Guru Nanak's
first udasi ended at Jagannath Puri. From here, Nanak
and Mardana returned towards the village of Talwandi

and the town of Sultanpur. On the way, they travelled
through the wild and dangerous areas of central India.
Several stories are associated with this part of the travel,
including the amazing story of Kauda, the cannibal-
demon. This cannibal-demon seized Mardana and would
have proceeded to add him to his list of victims but for
Guru Nanak who came upon the scene and greeted him.
There was such benign tranquillity in the Guru's voice,
such peace and love that Kauda stopped in mid-track,
released Mardana and fell at the Guru's feet. Guru
Nanak and Mardana stayed with Kauda for seven days.

Mardana's hunger and associated panic kept
bothering him throughout the journey. Walking through
the jungles another day, he complained again to Guru
Nanak, 'I will die of this hunger; there is no way out of
this frightening jungle. Surely I will be eaten up by some
wild beast. There will be no one left to tell all the tales
of my travels to Rai Bular and Mehta Kalu.' Guru Nanak
asked Mardana to be patient and join him in singing a
hymn to God, but Mardana claimed that he did not
have the strength left in him to play the rabab. Guru
Nanak then told him to eat the fruit from an overhanging
branch. 'Eat all you want,' said the Guru, 'but carry
none with you.' Mardana however was tempted, not
only to eat his fill, but also to pack some for a later
time. However, when he tried to eat the fruit later, it
had lost its sweetness and only gave him an excruciating

stomach ache. He confessed his transgression to the Guru and begged him to deliver him from the failing of human hunger once and for all.

During their journey, Guru Nanak and Mardana came upon a village whose inhabitants did not welcome them. Rather, they mocked them and refused them any hospitality. Guru Nanak blessed the village as they left, 'May this village thrive.' In sharp contrast, when they came upon a village that warmly welcomed them, the Guru only said, 'May this village be deserted.' Mardana could not help expressing his shock, 'Where is the justice, O Master? Those who ill-treat us you bless and those who welcome us you wish to scatter.' But Guru Nanak had his reasons. He explained that the inhabitants of the first village should confine their habits to themselves while the good villagers should go in all directions so that others may emulate them.

When at last they reached the familiar countryside near Talwandi, Guru Nanak stopped and sat down in the forest, three miles outside the village, while Mardana hurried homewards to check out how his family had fared in his absence. The word that Mardana the *dum* had come back spread like wildfire through the village. Nanak's mother Tripta asked anxiously about her son. However, Mardana only said: 'I was with the Baba in Sultanpur. After that, I do not know where he went.' But Tripta took some clothes and sweets and followed

Mardana as he walked out of the village. Thus she came upon the spot where her son sat. Her husband soon followed her, riding to that spot on horseback. There followed a warm reunion of Guru Nanak with his parents. The entire village, including Rai Bular, gathered to listen to the Guru and to hear the tales of their travels from Mardana. Mehta Kalu and Tripta tried their best to make Nanak give up his travels and return to family life. But Guru Nanak sought their blessings for continuing on his journeys to comply with God's will.

On their way from Talwandi to Sultanpur, Guru Nanak and Mardana passed through Pakpattan, the ferry crossing over the Sutlej river. Pakpattan was famous as the town of Baba Farid, the thirteenth century-Muslim saint. Even Timur had spared the populace of this town out of respect for the saint who lay buried there. Nanak met with the sheikh's successor, Sheikh Ibrahim, and the two had long spiritual discourses on the nature of God and worship. When Nanak had retired to rest and the sheikh was still in meditation, a villager left a bowl of milk for the two holy men and secretly slipped four gold mohurs in it. The sheikh poured out his share of milk and drank it. In the morning, he offered the rest to Nanak, saying triumphantly, 'Those who keep awake obtain God's bounty.'

The Guru replied, 'Of God's ways none can tell.

Some miss his blessing when they are awake, others are woken up and overwhelmed with gifts.' He then showed the sheikh the four mohurs that lay at the bottom of the bowl. When the villager came back for his bowl, he found that it had been turned into gold and was full of gold mohurs. He regretted that he had not wished for something greater from the men of God, perhaps salvation.

In 1509, Guru Nanak returned to Sultanpur, to his wife and sons, to sister Nanaki and Jairam. He had been thirteen years on the road.

As Far as the Land
Stretched . . .

Before proceeding on his second udasi, the Guru left Sultanpur and took the ferry across the Beas river at Goindwal. Coming upon a village on the north bank, he stood at the doorway of a lone hut that was a little away from the village. This was the hut of a faqir suffering from leprosy, who was ostracized by the rest of the village. Nanak requested the faqir to let him spend the night in the hut. The leper was astounded. 'Even beasts run away from me,' he said, 'I am indeed blessed that you should come here.' Nanak then recited the *shabad* contained in the Granth Sahib:

> The soul burns in agony and burning, loses its
> way repeatedly.
> The body that forgets the Lord's Name
> Screams like a real leper.
> To speak is in vain
> For the Creator already knows everything.
> . . . worldly attachments are the real scars
> The one who departs from this world
> With the scars of sin on his face
> Finds no place in the Lord's court.
> —Raga Dhanasari

The faqir was cured of his illness and fell at the Guru's feet.

Passing through the villages of Vairowal, Jalalabad

and the Muslim village of Kiri Pathana, Nanak once again entered Lahore. A wealthy merchant by the name of Dhuni Chand welcomed him to his house. Elaborate ceremonies were taking place in the house on the occasion of the death anniversary of the merchant's father. Brahmins were being fed rich delicacies in the belief that the food would reach the departed spirit. Guru Nanak noticed that seven flags were fastened on Dhuni Chand's door and asked him as to what they signified.

'Each one of them signifies one lakh rupees; together they signify the fortune I have collected in this world.'

Upon hearing that, Nanak gave Dhuni Chand a needle and said, 'I am giving this to you for safe keeping. I will take it from you in the next world.'

The puzzled merchant took the needle to his wife and told her what the Guru had said. 'Go back and return the needle to the Guru,' she said. 'Who takes anything from this world when he departs?'

Dhuni Chand got the message. Neither could he take his wealth with him nor would the food being fed to the Brahmins reach his father. If he gave to the needy in the name of the Lord, the merit of the good deed would go with him.

The Guru then came to the ancient town of Sialkot where he meditated under a ber tree at the edge of a graveyard. The place is even today known as Babe di Ber. He learnt that a Muslim pir, Shah Hamzah was bent on destroying the entire city because he was angry with one of its inhabitants named Ganga. Ganga, who had been childless, had sought the blessings of Shah and had promised to give him one of the children born to him. But when he became the father of three children he was unwilling to give up any of them. Shah Hamzah had cursed that the entire city be destroyed for that reason and was now fasting for forty days to make his curse come true. When the faqir emerged after his penance of forty days and went to see Guru Nanak, he was told to desist from destroying the entire city as it surely would have some good persons too. To prove this, Nanak wrote 'falsehood' and 'truth' on two slips of paper, and giving them to Mardana with two paise, told him to go to the town and purchase the two commodities. Mardana went from shop to shop but those who saw the slips were only puzzled by his demand. At last one shopkeeper named Mula took the slips of paper and wrote on one: 'Death is the truth,' and on the other: 'Life is false.' The Guru showed the piece of paper to the pir and convinced him that as long as people like Bhai Mula existed in Sialkot, the town should not be destroyed for the breach of promise by one of its inhabitants.

Probably in 1510, Guru Nanak was ready to undertake his second long journey, this time to the south. According to the Puratan janamsakhi, he was accompanied by two Jats, Saido and Gheho, although Mardana too is mentioned at places. He crossed the Sutlej near Bhatinda, and according to the diaries of wandering Bhatts or minstrels, he spent more than four months in Sirsa with Sufi saints, convincing them of the superiority of compassion and piety over the use of occult powers. Moving into Rajasthan, Nanak visited the Jain monks of the Dhundia sect at Bikaner. He preached that life and death, suffering and joy were matters that were in the hands of the Lord and it was a sin to live in the darkness of superstition.

At Ajmer, Nanak discoursed with Sufi leaders at the dargah of the revered Khwaja Muin-ud-din Chisti. In guiding the pirs on the true nature of their mission in life, he said:

> Lust is the devil, wrath is forbidden, the world
> is unreal,
> Truth is for the dervish, justice for the monarch,
> mercy for the faqir.

Just four miles away lay Pushkar, famous even today for its mela. There Nanak preached his message to those who had gathered to celebrate Baisakhi, the harvest festival of northern India. Thereafter Guru Nanak set his course clearly for the south, passing through several towns including Abu, Ujjain, Indore,

Hoshangabad, Amravati, Hingoli, Bidar, Golconda, Ganpur, Guntoor, Arcot, Pondicherry, Tiruchchirappalli and Rameshwaram. Old gurdwaras exist at many of the above towns, notably Rameshwaram and Guntoor. He sailed across to Sri Lanka and is believed to have landed at the Sri Lankan port of Trincomalee. Close to Trincomalee is the old port of Mattiakulam, later changed by the Dutch to Batticaloa. During his stay in Sri Lanka, Nanak spent most of his time in the vicinity of this town. Recently discovered local traditions in a small village called Kurukul Mandal near Batticaloa trace their origin to the visit of a jagat guru, or world teacher, some five centuries ago.

According to the janamsakhis, there was a raja named Shivnabh in Sri Lanka at that time. In Shivnabh's territory lived a trader called Mansukh, who had once been a jeweller in Lahore and was influenced by Guru Nanak's teachings. Shivnabh soon learnt that Mansukh did not follow traditional Hindu rituals—he did not worship idols, keep fasts or observe other religious austerities. Instead, he would rise before dawn, bathe in cold water, and then recite the Japji of Nanak. After the sun rose, he would go about his worldly business, and in the evening he again sang the hymns of his Guru. When Shivnabh desired to know more about these beliefs, Mansukh explained that the sight of an exalted being, a man called Nanak, had freed him from the

practice of meaningless ritual and put him on the path
to salvation. Shivnabh was curious to meet Nanak.
Mansukh assured him that should he wish it in his heart,
Guru Nanak would surely visit him. Soon Shivnabh's
curiosity turned into an ardent desire to meet Guru
Nanak. Finally, one day he was informed that a holy
man and his companions had come to his gardens.
Shivnabh thought that perhaps what Mansukh had said
had indeed come true. To ascertain whether this man
was truly the Guru that he sought, Shivnabh first sent
beautiful dancing girls to dance before the Guru. The
Guru was not distracted and remained lost in meditation.
Then Shivnabh came down himself and posed several
questions to Nanak. Among these, he asked him whether
he followed the Muslim or the Hindu way of life.
Nanak's reply was:

> The True Guru has solved the problem of the
> two paths
> He who meditates on the One God and wavers
> not, shall understand.

—Raga Maru

Nanak talked at length to Shivnabh and his wife
about the ways of God and the mystery of existence.
The Raja had himself long pondered the eternal
questions, troubled as he was by his unfulfilled yearning

for a son. During the Guru's stay, Raja Shivnabh and his wife looked after him like true disciples. After the Guru left, their fervent wish for a child was fulfilled and a son was born to them.

It was during his stay of more than two years in Sri Lanka that Nanak is said to have composed the 'Pransangali', a poem in twenty-one stanzas that describes the true religious reality—the supreme state in which there is no rejoicing or mourning, no hopes or desires. However, the authenticity of this composition is disputed, which is why it is not included in the Adi Granth. Nanak also travelled to other parts of the country—Katargama, Sitawaka, Mannar and Anuradhapura where a preserved inscription, also disputed, refers to him as Jnanakacarya.

The return journey of the second udasi took Nanak and his companions along the western ghats, including towns such as Nasik, Ankla, Baroda, Junagadh, Dwarka, Bhuj, and finally back to Rajputana and Punjab. When they reached the outskirts of Multan, they were met by a delegation of Sufi pirs. They offered Guru Nanak a cup of milk, full to the brim. The implication of this gesture was that in Multan, known for its pirs and saints, including the descendants of Sheikh Bahauddin Zakaria, there was no place for one more holy man. The Guru, it is said, took a jasmine petal and let it float gently on the surface of the milk, implying that his presence would not uproot anyone. The discourses that he then proceeded to hold with the pirs showed them the path to humility and self-knowledge.

Nanak once again returned to Talwandi to the extreme joy of his ageing parents. Rai Bular was in his last days and Nanak's presence at his bedside proved to be a source of great peace and comfort. Then, probably in the year 1515, Guru Nanak returned to Sultanpur.

And Then He Climbed
Sumer . . .

Sultanpur had strong claims on Guru Nanak—the love and affection of sister Nanaki and her husband, Jairam, the high regard of Governor Daulat Khan Lodhi, the memories, friendships and attachments founded in the years he had worked and meditated there. But Guru Nanak's wandering days were not yet over. Probably in the summer of 1517, he set out once again with Mardana, this time to the north.

But before he left for the mountains, he made a trip to Majha, the area of Punjab that lies between the rivers Ravi and Beas. A piece of land on the bank of the Ravi attracted his attention and he decided to make that his eventual home. According to one version, it is said that one of his disciples Ajita Randhawa, along with some other farmers, pledged that piece of land to the Guru. Here, probably in the beginning of 1516, Guru Nanak founded the community that he called Kartarpur, the city of the creator.

The news of the Guru's presence at Kartarpur spread fast. People of all creeds, castes and ranks—Hindus and Muslims, yogis, householders, noblemen and ordinary peasants—came to seek his blessings. Among the people who came there was a wealthy man called Karoria, or figuratively speaking, one who is worth ten million rupees. He was troubled by the thought that Nanak was trying to misguide both Hindus and Muslims, and decided to go to Kartarpur to stop the activities of Guru

Nanak. But when he mounted his horse, the horse would not move. When he tried again the next day, he could not see anything. The people around him told him that Nanak was a great pir, and that the nobleman should take his name with reverence. Karoria began to praise the Guru, but when he sought to mount his horse again and ride towards him he was blinded and fell from the horse. Thereafter, Karoria proceeded on foot towards the Guru, and falling at his feet, received his gracious blessings. Karoria became one of the disciples who helped Guru Nanak in settling Kartarpur. Ultimately as the settlement expanded, the Guru's parents and family, along with the family of his companion, Mardana, came to live in Kartarpur.

For the journey to the north, Nanak dressed differently, perhaps keeping in mind the extreme weather he was to encounter. He wore leather on his feet and on his head, and wound a rope around his body. Guru Nanak travelled widely in the Himalayas and several scholars have constructed possible routes that he could have taken, based on the local traditions still extant in the mountains and the gurdwaras that have been founded down the centuries. The route taken by Guru Nanak may vary from scholar to scholar but legend has traced his footsteps to Himachal Pradesh, Jammu and Kashmir, Uttar Pradesh, Sikkim, Ladakh and even Nepal and Tibet. The central event of the third udasi is the visit to Mount Sumer, recorded by all the janamsakhis and by Bhai Gurdas. Mount Sumer is none other than Mount Kailash, the venerated abode of Shiva and Parvati.

The long and arduous journey began by crossing the Sutlej near the camp of a venerated pir, Budhan Shah. A town called Kiratpur was later founded at this place by the sixth Sikh Guru, Hargobind. Today, Kiratpur is a small peaceful settlement at the entrance to the Shivalik hills where the Sutlej flows gently among vast open fields. The Guru's climb through the mountains took him to Rawalsar, Kangra, Mandi and Kulu. Guru Nanak is also believed to have visited the settlement of Manikaran, in the narrow valley of the choppy Parbati river. There, in the old gurdwara, the langar, or the food of the community kitchen, is cooked not on any fire but in the steam that rises from the boiling hot springs at the very edge of the ice-cold river. Local tradition also says that Nanak passed over the Chandrakhani pass and went down to the village of Malana in a steep rock bowl, the home of an ancient community that generally does not welcome outsiders.

Guru Nanak then travelled through the dramatic and barren stretches of Spiti Valley. He traversed the Shipki-la pass and then moved towards the Lipu Lekh pass to enter the region of Gangotri and Kedar Kshetra. From here he followed the ancient routes that have led pilgrims for centuries to the lake Mansarovar, the source of the Sutlej, at the feet of the holy mountain of Kailash. Mount Kailash stands at 22,000 feet above sea level and pilgrims take almost three days to perform its circumambulation. Among Mount Kailash and the crystal-clear waters of Mansarovar and Rakas Tal is based the famous meeting of Nanak with the eighty-four Siddhas, among them the ancient Gorakhnath, Machendranath and Charpat Nath, or perhaps the successors of these famous ancient souls, who had meditated deep and long and possessed great power and wisdom.

In Bhai Gurdas's version of the meeting, the Siddhas expressed amazement at seeing Nanak. 'O youthful one! What power brings you to these heights? Who is it that you worship?'

'The eternal lord alone,' replied Nanak.

The Siddhas asked him how the world below was faring. Guru Nanak made no secret of what he felt. He told them that darkness, sin and injustice had taken over the world. Corruption was rampant; the fence itself had begun to eat the crop. The wise Siddhas had escaped into remote caves. Who then would redeem the world?

The Siddhas argued that it was not possible to be part of the world and follow the path of meditation and spirituality. Nanak replied that one had to be 'as a lotus in the water that remaineth dry'. One had to meditate on God's name and remain unaffected by the world.

Attempting to lure Nanak from his path so that he may join their fold, the Siddhas asked him to bring water in a yogi's bowl from the lake. When he reached the lake he found rubies, diamonds and other precious stones in the water. He went back empty-handed and told the Siddhas that the lake had no water in it. When they came down to check, it was true. The lake had indeed dried up. The ancients recognized Nanak's genius and acknowledged him as a spiritual master.

After this the Guru travelled widely in Tibet as is manifested by strong local traditions. In fact there is a view that some Buddhists revere Nanak as an emanation of Lord Padmasambhava or the Bhadra Guru. Rewalsar is holy to both Sikhs and Buddhists, and Buddhist lamas can often be seen travelling to Amritsar to honour Rimpoche Nanak (the reincarnate one).

According to some local legends and accounts, Nanak went further east—into Sikkim and Nepal. In Nepal, Nanak want to Janakpur, the fabled birthplace of Sita. He moved along to the Dhomri fort and preached the worship of one God at the fair of Brahmkund. Ultimately, Nanak *rishi*, as he was known in Nepal, arrived at Kathmandu and stayed near the Pashupatinath temple on the bank of the Bhagmati river. Singing hymns to the tune of Mardana's rabab, Nanak captivated the people of Kathmandu, including the king. Even today,

a gurdwara with the impression of the Guru's feet stands
on a hillock in the city. Nanak's journeys in Nepal took
him to the several major temples of the Hindu kingdom
and possibly to the Thyangboche monastery which is
picturesquely placed at the base of Mount Everest. In
Sikkim, a huge boulder in the village of Chung Thang,
at the confluence of the Teesta and Lachung Chu is said
to mark the place where Rimpoche Nanak Guru stopped
in his travels before moving on to Chumbi Valley of
Tibet. The boulder was thrown at him by a demon but
only fell at the Guru's feet. The Guru's footprints can
be seen in the rock and the boulder is known as 'Pathar
Sahib'. His footprints are also preserved at the Lachen
Monastery on the way to Gurudongman Lake. Legends
of his travels abound in this area and there is even a
gurdwara called Nanak Lama Sahib.

On his return from Tibet, Nanak entered Ladakh
from the Chasul pass and rested at the Hemis Gompa,
where a stone still marks the place of the Guru's repose.
Passing through Leh, he took the path to Kargil. On
this road is a rock with the impression of the head and
torso of an ogre said to have been chastised by the Guru
when it tried to frighten his companions. The impression
of the Guru's footsteps can be found in Skardu in
Baltistan and in Srinagar in the Kashmir Valley where
he visited the temple of Sankaracharya. Guru Nanak

also visited the Amarnath caves, scene of the traditional Hindu pilgrimage, and preached his message to devotees who were performing the traditional Amarnath yatra. Gurdwara Mattan Sahib commemorates his visit to Amarnath. It was near the town of Mattan, forty miles to the east of Srinagar, that he met Pandit Brahm Das. During the ensuing dialogue, the learned pandit, armed with two camel loads of Sanskrit books, questioned Nanak closely and attacked his manner of dress. Nanak then led him into a discussion of creation and the existence of the true lord before creation. According to Puratan janamsakhi, Nanak brought home to Brahm Das the emptiness of maya in a rather unique way. Though Brahm Das had ostensibly understood Nanak's teachings and agreed to follow the path of God, his heart was not yet fully convinced. One day Guru Nanak asked him to take a Guru. 'Where should I find one?' asked Brahm Das. Nanak pointed towards a hut where four faqirs lived. When Brahm Das went there, the faqirs pointed towards a temple where he should go to seek a Guru. When Brahm Das reached the temple, he was severely beaten with a shoe by a woman who was guarding the temple. Brahm Das went back to the faqirs and told his pathetic tale to them. 'That was Maya,' they said, 'she is your Guru.' Brahm Das then came and fell at Nanak's feet and threw away his load of books.

Now Guru Nanak passed through Jammu and

headed homewards. At Sultanpur, his doting sister Nanaki passed away suddenly, and three days later, her husband, Jairam, too succumbed to a fever. There was little in Sultanpur to hold him back, and Guru Nanak soon set off on his fourth great journey, this time to the Muslim countries that lay to the west of India.

And Then the Baba Went to Mecca . . .

For this journey to the Muslim countries, Nanak adorned a blue dress, and in the manner of a Haji, carried with him a staff, a book, a cup and a prayer rug. He was accompanied by Mardana as before. Once again Guru Nanak reached Multan and then the town of Sukkur on the western bank of the Indus. Crossing the Habb river, Nanak moved into Baluchistan where he paid a visit to the famous shrine of Hinglaj, tucked away between mountain ranges and dedicated to the Hinglaj Devi, also known as Bibi Nani to Muslims and Parvati or Kali to Hindus. He held a discourse here with Vaishnavite ascetics who were confounded by his manner of dress and could not make out to which faith he paid obeisance.

Coming down from the hills, he joined a group of pilgrims and set sail for Mecca from the port of Miani. Passing the port of Aden, the pilgrims probably disembarked at the port of Al Aswadh on the Red Sea, off Jeddah, from where Mecca was not too far. Joining a slow moving camel caravan of pilgrims performing the holiest journey of their lives, Guru Nanak and Mardana crossed forty miles of desert wilderness to reach that ancient town.

As night fell in the holy city, Guru Nanak laid down to rest with his feet pointing towards the Ka'aba. When Rukn-ud-din, the Qazi came to the shrine to say his evening prayers, he saw the pilgrim sleeping in that fashion and berated him, 'Why do you commit such infidelity? Do you not know that there is the house of God, the Ka'aba? How dare you point your feet in that direction?'

Nanak replied, 'Then O Qazi, point my feet in the direction where there is no God.'

The Qazi held Nanak's legs and turned his feet around. But to his amazement, say the janamsakhis, he found the Ka'aba turning around too. No matter what direction he would point Nanak's feet, the Ka'aba too would turn. Guru Nanak had made his point. God, the creator, is omnipresent.

Thereafter, the wise men of Mecca, the Qazis and the Mullahs, the pilgrims and the devotees, gathered to discourse over religious issues with Nanak. They questioned him about the relative merits of Hinduism and Islam. According to Bhai Gurdas, Nanak replied that without good action, all were doomed. Without good deeds, the external guises would not stand up in God's court; they would be washed away like the colour of the kasumbha flower is washed away by water. Though Ram and Rahim were one, the true God had been forgotten and the world was being led by the devil.

Nanak and Mardana then headed to the second holy city, Medina, where news of Nanak's discourses in Mecca had already reached before them. Here too Nanak held religious discussions with learned Imams.

Though some accounts claim that Nanak went on to visit Palestine, Syria and Turkey, it is more generally accepted that from Medina, Guru Nanak turned eastwards and walked across the blazing sandy wastes to Baghdad on the banks of the Tigris river. An inscription in stone discovered in the city by a Sikh army officer during the First World War appears to mention the Guru's name.

Baghdad was then a great centre of Islamic learning, art and culture. On the outskirts of the great city, in a graveyard, Mardana strummed the strings of his rabab in holy melody and Nanak sang holy hymns. In the orthodox Islamic setting this was considered a sacrilege, but when the townspeople came out to throw stones at the itinerant infidel, Nanak concluded his prayers with the call, 'Sat Kartar' in a divinely captivating voice and the crowd was stunned into silence.

The Pir-e-Dastgir of Baghdad came out to meet Nanak and inquired what faith he belonged to and what sect of faqirs he came from. It was Mardana who replied, 'Nanak has come to this world in Kalyug, the horrible cosmic age. He has rejected all faqirs except the supreme being, who is all pervasive—in the heavens, the earth and all four directions.'

During his stay in Baghdad, the Guru also met another pir known as Bahlol who had several discourses with him. Finally, Bahlol and his son became followers

of Nanak. The devotion of Bahlol to Nanak is expressed
in a beautiful poem written in the twentieth century by
an itinerant Hindu monk, Swami Anand Acharya, after
visiting the legendary place of the meeting. To quote
just a couple of verses from this poem:

What peace from Himalaya's lonely
    caves and forests thou didst carry
    to the vine-groves and rose-gardens
    of Baghdad!
What light from Badrinath's snowy
    peak thou didst bear to illumine
    the heart of Balol, thy saintly
    Persian disciple!
Eight fortnights Balol hearkened to
    thy words on life and the Path
    and Spring Eternal, while the moon
    waxed and waned in the pomegranate grove
    beside the grassy desert of the dead . . .

    —Sri Ananda Acharya: 'On reading an Arabic
    inscription in a shrine outside the town of
    Baghdad, dated 912 Hejira' in Snowbirds,
    London, Macmillan 1919.

Guru Nanak stayed in Baghdad for about four months.
A shrine in Baghdad, also known as the tomb of Bahlol,

marks the visit of Guru Nanak and his association with Bahlol.

From Baghdad, the Guru probably entered Iran through the traditional route that passed through Kermanshah and has been followed for centuries by Muslim pilgrims visiting or returning from Karbala and Najaf. The exact route that Nanak and Mardana followed has been covered up by the passing centuries but local traditions lead us to believe that they probably passed through Tehran, Isfahan and Mashad, where Nanak held discussions with top Shia leaders. From there he went along the Amu Darya and reached Bukhara, and thereafter continued the journey through Afghanistan, visiting several places including Balkh, Kabul, Kandahar and Mazar-i-Sharif before crossing back into India through the Khyber pass. In Peshawar, at a place called Gorakhatri, Nanak had a discourse with the yogis of the *kanphata* sect.

When they had crossed the Indus and were passing the town of Hassan Abdal, Mardana was overcome with fatigue and thirst. On the top of a nearby hill lived a Muslim saint, Baba Wali Kandahari who guarded a reservoir of fresh water. When Mardana told Wali that he was accompanying Nanak, another exalted pir, Wali Kandahari refused to give him any water, saying that if his master was so powerful, he should be able to give Mardana some water. Mardana went back to Guru

Nanak and related what had transpired. Nanak told him to go back and beseech Wali again. Mardana did so but his efforts failed to move the adamant Wali. Guru Nanak then asked Mardana to lift a small stone from the hillside. As Mardana did so, a spring of fresh water gushed forth. Mardana drank to his heart's content. The new spring however began to drain Wali's reservoir on top of the hill. In anger, Wali is said to have hurled a boulder at Guru Nanak. The Guru stopped the boulder with his outstretched palm, leaving the impression of his hand on the rock. This rock, the bubbling spring and the legend of Wali Kandahari are preserved at the venerated Sikh gurdwara at Panja Sahib.

Towards the end of 1520, Babar's murderous hordes came charging into Punjab for the third time. They first moved towards Sialkot and that major town succumbed to the invaders without a fight. They then turned their edgy horses towards Saidpur, and sensing defiance, began to sack the town. Guru Nanak was at that time returning from his fourth udasi and had reached Saidpur to meet his old disciple, Lalo. He saw the cruelty of Babar and his men, and the intense suffering of the innocent people, men and women, Muslims and Hindus alike. The pain in his soul found its way into the *Babar Vani*, the beautiful poetry of protest and pain that is now contained in the Granth Sahib.

The Puratan janamsakhi relates a meeting between

Babar and Guru Nanak though the Babarnamah does not have any mention of such a meeting. According to the janamsakhi, Nanak and Mardana were captured by Babar's forces and taken to prison. Nanak was asked to carry a load and Mardana to lead a horse. But the soldiers noticed that the load carried itself and the horse followed Mardana of its own free will. In the prison, like the other prisoners, the Guru too was given a mill and asked to grind corn. The guards saw that as the Guru meditated, the mill turned of its own accord. When this was reported to Babar, he came to see the faqir. It is said that the invader touched the Guru's feet and offered gifts to the dervish. But Guru Nanak refused to take anything. He instead asked Babar to release all the prisoners and return their property to them. Babar complied, and from Saidpur Nanak moved on to Kartarpur.

Kartarpur

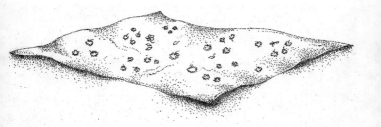

At Kartarpur, Nanak took off his travel garb and wore the ordinary clothes of a householder. He had travelled for more than two decades in all directions. He had met and talked to all kinds of people and dispelled as he went along the forces of darkness, the mists of superstition and the overpowering confines of ritual. He had spread far his message of true love, equality and compassion, truth and truthful living. He had explained through his discourses the all-pervasive, timeless nature of the creator. Now it was time to show in practical terms that renunciation and asceticism were not the answer to life's challenge. True religious discipline had to be forged while living in the world, amidst all its challenges and temptations, troubles and joys.

The community at Kartarpur grew steadily. Men of all callings and faiths—householders and ascetics, destitute mendicants and wealthy merchants, Brahmins and dervishes, Hindus and Muslims, came there, drawn by the message of piety and humanity. A number of traditions were started at Kartarpur, in particular the traditions of kirtan and langar.

Mardana, who had played his rabab in tune with the Guru's hymns in faraway places, played the rabab at Kartarpur too. Prayers from the Guru's compositions were recited at different hours of the day—the Japji and the *Asa di Var* in the early hours of the morning, the

Sodar in the evenings, and the *Sohila* before retiring. The Guru's shabads, or hymns, were sung in chorus. Thus was born the tradition of kirtan, the singing of divine compositions usually by a congregation of devotees (sangat) that induces a mood of contemplation of God's name.

The Kartarpur community started the great Sikh tradition of langar, the community kitchen where the rich and poor eat the same food together, irrespective of social standing or caste or rank. Langar symbolizes brotherhood and encourages humility. Men and women vie with each other in its preparation, be it the cutting of vegetables, making chapattis, serving the food or cleaning up the leaf platters. All the tasks are considered sewa, or voluntary physical service for the good of the community.

But the idea of langar was initially not accepted readily by everyone. The Puratan janamsakhi tells the tale of a Brahmin who came to visit the Guru but refused to eat food cooked in the common kitchen. He wanted to dig up the earth, make his own hearth, clean his firewood and consecrate his kitchen before cooking his food. Unfortunately for him, no matter where he began to dig, he found only bones. Finally, tired and hungry, he came back to Guru Nanak and requested that he be given food. The Guru's *bani* captures it as follows:

The hearth may be paved with gold,
Of gold be the pots and pans,
And the vast square be marked with silver lines,
The water be from the Ganges,
The firewood from the yajnas,
And the food fine rice boiled in milk;
These are all of no account, my soul
If the True Name does not absorb thee.

—Raga Basant

A number of close and faithful disciples gathered around the Guru at Kartarpur. Some of their names are mentioned by Bhai Gurdas in one of his vars: Bhai Budda, Taru Popat and Moola Keer. Taru Popat was but a child of ten when he came to Guru Nanak and sought his blessings. Nanak observed that he was young and wondered how he had learnt the right way so early in life. Popat replied that he had once seen a fire being lit by his mother. He had noticed that the smaller logs always caught fire before the big logs. So it would be easier for him, as a child, to find a Guru and seek the path to salvation. Guru Nanak gave him the name of Taru, meaning a swimmer who would carry himself and his followers across the troubled waters of existence.

Moola Keer was another disciple who gained the Guru's love by his belief in the honour of his faith. He treated all who came to his house with love, and offered them food and a bed to rest. One day a Sikh who knew much of the scriptures but had not absorbed the message came to his house. When Moola and his wife had retired for the night, the guest picked up the wife's gold ornaments. In the morning, Moola opened the door to bid his guest goodbye, but as the man was leaving the house, the bag of the ornaments dropped and the gold bangles fell on the ground. Moola picked them up, put them in the bag, gave the bag to the guest and bade him farewell. When his wife could not find her ornaments, Moola told her that a thief must have broken into the house and taken the ornaments away. Then he had new ornaments made for his wife. He resorted to all this simply because he did not wish that anyone who called himself a Sikh should be associated with such a deed.

Baba Budda, who lived up to the age of 125 years, was only a twelve-year-old boy called Bura when Guru Nanak found him in a field, grazing his cattle. He brought the Guru a bowl of milk and requested him, 'I am fortunate to have seen you. Deliver me now from the endless circuit of life and death.' The Guru told him that he was but a child and asked him the source of his wisdom. Bura replied that he had once seen a group of soldiers mowing down ripe as well as unripe crops with their swords. He had then thought that the hand of death could also deliver the young and the old alike. Why not then seek salvation when young? The Guru was

impressed that Bura spoke not as a child but as a wise
old man. That is how Bura acquired the name of Budda,
the old man. Baba Budda lived to see five Sikh Gurus
and became one of the most respected members of the
community. When the Granth Sahib was first installed
in the Hari Mandir Sahib at Amritsar in 1604, Bhai
Budda was appointed the first Granthi, or custodian of
the book.

It was at Kartarpur that Lehna, who was to later
become the second Sikh Guru, Angad Dev, came to
Nanak. Lehna, who belonged to Khadur village, was a
worshipper of the goddess Durga and used to lead an
annual procession to the Jawalamukhi temple. In his
village lived a man called Jodha who was a follower of
Guru Nanak. One day Lehna heard the Sikh sing the
Guru's hymns. He was deeply touched by the hymns
and yearned to meet Guru Nanak. On his next trip to
Jawalamukhi, Lehna stopped at Kartarpur for a meeting
with the Guru.

The Guru asked him his name.

'Lehna,' he replied.

'You had to receive your debt from here. That is
why you have come.' (In Punjabi, Lehna means the credit
that one has to receive.)

Lehna did not go to Jawalamukhi temple to worship
the goddess but stayed on at Kartarpur. He became an
obedient and humble disciple who ceaselessly performed

all the service that he could for the community. After three years, having attained tranquillity and peace, he went back to his village where he was greeted with reverence by his kinsman. Lehna, however, was soon to return to Kartarpur and once there, he went to meet Guru Nanak in the fields. There he volunteered to pick up a load of grass on his head. The mud dripped from the grass on to his fine clothes. Bebe Sulakhani asked Guru Nanak, 'Why is it that one from such a good family, with such nice clothes should carry a load of wet grass on his head?'

'This is not wet grass,' replied Nanak. 'It is the tiara of sovereignty.'

When Guru Nanak had reached the age of sixty-one, he, along with some disciples including Bhai Lehna, made a short trip across the Ravi to Achal near Batala on the occasion of Shivratri. They met a large gathering of holy men, acrobats, musicians, yogis and Siddhas. When the devotees who had gathered on the occasion heard of Guru Nanak's arrival, they surged forward to meet him. Angry at this, the Siddhas began to question and taunt Guru Nanak.

One of them, Bhangar Nath, questioned his apparent worldliness. 'Why did you give up your religious clothes and wear those of the world? Your action is like adding vinegar to milk and souring it.' Nanak replied that in their case, the butter had gone rancid since the churning vessels had been dirty. They had turned into ascetics and yet went begging to households for food. This only angered the Siddhas further. According to the janamsakhis, in their anger, some Siddhas became lions, others flew like birds, some turned into serpents while others brought down a rain of fire. Guru Nanak sat through this demonstration calmly and proclaimed the power of the word over all such acts. Ultimately the Siddhas gave up and acknowledged that it was the supreme god who was the true force and could not be comprehended by performing miracles. The name of God was the only true miracle.

Meanwhile Mardana, the companion of Guru Nanak for forty-seven years, was becoming ill and weak. As his last moments drew near, the Guru asked Mardana what should be done with his mortal remains. Should his body be entombed? Mardana said that he had overcome the pride of his body. If the Guru was releasing his soul from the cage of his body, then why enclose the body itself in stone? Mardana then fixed his mind on God, the creator, and just before dawn the next day, passed from this world. Guru Nanak consigned his body to the Ravi river to the singing of hymns and prayers. Guru Nanak then asked Mardana's son Shahzada to take his father's place and accompany him as a musician thenceforth.

Guru Nanak knew that the time would soon come for him too to depart from the mortal world. But before that there was the need to anoint a successor, so that the message of God's name would not end with his own mortal life. Nanak's choice fell not on either of his sons but on Lehna, the devoted and humble disciple. In a simple ceremony, Guru Nanak put five copper coins and a coconut before Lehna and gave him the name of Angad, part of his own limb. Baba Budda put the saffron tilak on Lehna's forehead. This established that Guruship among the Sikhs would not necessarily be hereditary; the torch would pass to the one most akin in spirit and not in blood. Secondly, the community of Sikhs would not be a community of ascetics or those who had renounced the world, like Sri Chand, Guru Nanak's elder son. It would be a community of householders, a religion that sought to live in the real world, on its own terms.

When finally the time came for the Guru to depart from this mortal world, he went and sat under an acacia tree. The withered tree was touched by sudden spring, sprouting new leaves and flowers. The Guru's disciples, both Hindu and Muslim, gathered around him. Guru Nanak asked them not to despair or weep. He reminded them that this was the way of all flesh:

O brethren, remember the Lord,
For all have to pass this way.

—Raga Wadhans

As he lay down to prepare for eternal repose, the
sangat sang the *Kirtan Sohila:*

Where the Lord's praise is sung,
And where men contemplate on Him,
Sing there the song of praise
And remember the Maker.

Praise then thou my Fearless Lord,
I sacrifice myself for the song that brings
Eternal comfort.

Day after day, the Great Giver
Watches over His Creation,
Cares for one and all.

The gifts of the Lord are priceless;
How then can we estimate the Giver?
The date and year of marriage is written;
Together pour, the oil of welcome
At the threshold

Give me your blessings, O friends,
That I may unite with my Master

The writ goes from house to house,
The summons arrive everyday,

Remember then the One who calls,
Nanak, the day is not far away.

The Guru then covered himself with a sheet and his soul departed its mortal confines. His Muslim and Hindu disciples began to argue over the manner of disposal of his remains. The Muslims said that he had been their pir so he should be buried; the Hindus, on the other hand, claimed his body for cremation. It was then decided by the wise men of both religions that flowers be kept besides his body by both groups, and the group whose flowers remained fresh in the morning may claim him. But when morning came, the flowers offered by the Hindus were as fresh as those offered by the Muslims, and when they removed the sheet that covered the body, they found only flowers. Even in his act of departing his mortal form, the messenger had left his message. Truly it is said:

Nanak the pious
Guru to the Hindu, Pir to the Mussalman.

The Teachings

Every year, when the birthday of Guru Nanak is celebrated in countless gurdwaras on Kartik Purnima, the congregations inevitably sing the shabad contained in the first var of Bhai Gurdas:

> When Guru Nanak appeared in this world
> The mists lifted, there was light everywhere,
> Like, with the rising of the sun
> Stars hide and darkness retreats,
> Like, at the roaring of a lion
> The deer flee . . .
>
> —Var 1, 27

Bhai Gurdas's verse contains two important pointers regarding Guru Nanak's mission on earth. First, the society into which Nanak was born, the world that he inherited, was in dire need of redemption. There was much that was wrong. There was ignorance and sin, corruption and oppression. Men had forgotten the way to salvation; the eternal truths had been lost in empty ritualism and blind superstition. External manifestations of religion were all that mattered; caste and sect ruled the life of men; the guardians of faith had become the oppressors. Those who tired of the world looked for a way out in its renunciation.

Secondly, Guru Nanak arrived in such a world as a redeemer. He was armed with a divine mission and he spoke as a divine witness, 'As the Lord sends his Word, so do I deliver it, O Lalo.' He was sensitive to the prevailing situation, the chaos and the confusion. He was unsparing in his criticism, often laced with sarcasm and humour, of the moral decay that had set in and of those who were responsible for it—kings and officials, godmen and yogis, Brahmins and Qazis. His mission was to dispel ignorance, contradict falsehood and impart a practical and ethical direction to religion. His audience did not belong to one particular religion or sect; the world was his canvas and his message was for all mankind. For in his view, all men were truly equal. His teachings were not a condemnation of any religion; rather, they were intended to underline the verities of tolerance and humanism inherent in each religion and remove the distortions. Guru Nanak's philosophy advocated an approach to life that seamlessly combines belief, thought and action. He put forward this philosophy in a myriad ways—through his own example, through his tireless travels, through his discourses with the learned men of all faiths, through the community that evolved around him at Kartarpur and perhaps, most of all, through his hymns, sung in praise of the supreme reality.

To try and encapsulate this philosophy in a few pages would be an overly ambitious task and one doomed to be incomplete. A focus on some of the cardinal principles may provide a better alternative.

* The Mul Mantra, or the opening stanza of the *Japji*,
  encapsulates Guru Nanak's idea of the supreme
  reality. Here Nanak says that there is but one God
  and true is his name. He is the all-pervading creator,
  fearless, without any enemy, timeless, without birth,
  and self-existent. He can be realized only through
  God's own grace. In this fundamental creed, the Guru
  captures the sublime essentials of God, doing away
  with all that may come in the way of enlightenment.

* The creator created all existence. When He did it or
  how is not known, nor can the human mind know
  the extent of the creation. But this creation, this
  universe, this world is no dream. It is real. It changes,
  decays, dies and renews. God, the cherisher, sustains
  his creation through the ages.

* The spiritual evolution of the soul is possible in this
  world itself, salvation can be found in life. The various
  khands or stages of this evolution are: Dharma
  (righteousness), Jnana (knowledge), Saram (effort),
  Karm (grace) and Sach (truth). Man need not wait
  for heaven to seek deliverance or moksha. The jivan-
  mukta is one who finds deliverance in this world itself
  by good deeds or by God's grace. His grace can be
  attained through contemplation of his name, and the
  five evils that persist in man—lust, anger, greed,

attachment and ego—can be overcome.

* The spirit of affirmation is an essential aspect of Guru Nanak's teachings. The world is real, it is a part of God's creation. It has to be accepted as a reflection of divine purpose. Man's duty is to live in it in such a way that he lives above the impurities, that he improves the condition of fellow human beings by love and compassion, by service and devotion. Renunciation is emphatically rejected. The answer does not lie in withdrawal from this world, in wandering in jungles with the body smeared in ash or meditating in isolation in snowy retreats. Guru Nanak supported institutions like marriage, family and society, and brought them within the ambit of religion.

* The concept of the Guru finds frequent mention in the Sikh scriptures. It stands as much for the human preceptor as for God. The Guru acts as a guide who places the seeker on the right path to salvation, but the disciple must walk the hard way himself.

* Practical virtue is stressed rather than abstract piety. The exhortations are remarkable in their simplicity: Kirt karo (do work), Nam japo (meditate on his name) and Vand chako (share in charity). Service, love and devotion are the essentials. In the words of Dr Radhakrishnan, Guru Nanak believed in 'religion as realization, anubhava'.

* It follows naturally that Guru Nanak rejected
  formalism and orthodoxy in religion. Man's journey
  had to be inwards rather than in the form of
  ceremonial pilgrimages. He questioned the
  hypocritical cant that passed for religion and the
  hidebound practices that the ordinary populace
  endured from birth to death without thinking of the
  essential ethical issues involved. He stressed the
  uselessness of charms and mantras, idolatory and
  ceremony. His purpose was to liberate the human
  spirit from the clutches of the priestly classes and the
  various monastic orders whose vested interest lay in
  making religion abstruse. Naturally he drew the ire
  of the orthodoxy—the Brahmins, the Qazis, the
  Siddhas and hathayogis. His message, however, was
  aimed at the common masses, both Hindu as well as
  the Muslim populace.

* Guru Nanak underlined the essential equality of man
  and the irrelevance of the different castes, sects and
  religions that humanity was divided into. A man's
  standing was to be determined by the deeds that he
  performed. If there is only one creator, then how can
  the men he has created be different? For him, men
  fell only into two categories: Gurmukh (God-
  oriented) and Manmukh (self-oriented). Guru
  Nanak also protested against the prevalent beliefs
  which gave an inferior position in society to women

and eloquently defended a woman's contribution and status. The concept of langar that Guru Nanak started at Kartarpur in which all eat the same food together was a practical manifestation of his belief in the equality of men.

The Hymns

Guru Nanak transmitted his message to the world and to the generations that were to follow in the form of deeply philosophical and spiritual hymns. His delicate and powerful poetry was an appropriate and beautiful vehicle for singing the praises of the supreme reality that he had perceived, the boundless beauty of creation itself, his contempt for the empty ritualism that passed off as religion, and his pain at the suffering of his fellow beings at the hands of oppressors. Rich in metaphor and simile, evocative in their descriptions and eloquent in their expression, Nanak's verses are clearly the work of an exalted being.

What was also significant was that he also rejected the use of Sanskrit which had become the language of the elite, the Brahmins, and chose the common man's language, Punjabi, that obviated the need of the medium of a priest. At the same time, he did not hesitate to enrich the language with Persian and Arabic when he thought it appropriate. He used terms employed by Upanishads, Sufi saints, Siddhas and yogis. Yet the end result remains one that can be easily comprehended by the ordinary man—the farmer, the carpenter, the ascetic and the householder.

Guru Nanak's hymns along with the additions by the following Gurus formed the core of the Granth Sahib that was fashioned out by the fifth Sikh Guru, Arjan Dev in 1604. The Guru Granth Sahib comprises almost a 1000 verse-units under nineteen ragas. Of these, the long compositions are the *Japji*, *Siddha Gosht*, *Dakhni Onkar*, *Asa di Var*, *Majh di Var*, *Malhar di Var*, *Patti* and *Barah Mah Tukhari*. Other shorter but distinct banis include the *Sodar* (Rehras), *Sohila*, *Babar Vani* and *Alahunian*.

Japji

This composition, the masterpiece of Guru Nanak, contains the essence of Sikh philosophy and religion. It has been compared to the Gita and the New Testament in as much as it contains within itself the quintessential beliefs of an entire philosophy. In a remarkably succinct form—only thirty-eight hymns or pauris and two shlokas—the composition analyses the deepest of spiritual problems: the eternal problem of human salvation. In poetry of supreme achievement, in varying metres, rich with deep intellectual and descriptive content, Guru Nanak discusses the fundamental issues of existence and the relationship of the creation with its creator. He examines the religious and philosophical issues facing mankind and shows a path: the contemplation of the name of the supreme being. The wisdom of the seeker is not confined to meditative contemplation but leads to enlightened action. Unlike most of the other compositions in the holy Granth, the *Japji* is not set to music. Every Sikh is expected to recite the *Japji* in the early, ambrosial morning hours, when the mind is fresh and best attuned to a contemplation of the maker.

The *Japji* begins with the Mul Mantra (the Fundamental Creed), the incredibly expressive description of God or the eternal truth in a short series of sentence-phrases:

> There is but one God, true is His Name,
> The Creator, fearless, without rancour,
> Timeless, unborn, self-existent
> By God's grace He is known
> Meditate on Him
> He was true
> In the beginning, in the primal time,
> O Nanak, true He is and will be hereafter.

> Reflection, even a million fold
> Will not reveal Him
> Silence, deep in His love
> Will not bring peace
> The hungry do not lose their hunger for Him
> With all the world's valuables
> Not one of man's thousand wisdoms
> Will serve him in the Lord's court.
> How then can one be true?
> How to tear the screen of untruth?

O Nanak, by obeying His pre-ordained will.

By His command are all forms manifest
Inexpressible is His command
By His command are all beings created
By the same are some made great
By His command are they made high or low
By His command are they blessed or cursed
By His command some are graced
While others revolve in the cycle of birth and
death
All fall under His command
None is beyond it
O Nanak, if man were to understand His
command
Then he would not hold on to ego

Who can sing of His might? Who has the power?
Who can sing of His grace or His bounties?
Some sing of His noble attributes and
greatnesses
Who can sing of His knowledge, difficult to
comprehend?
Some sing how He makes the body and then
reduces it to dust
Some sing that He takes away life and then gives
it

Some say that He appears far away
Some say that He is always face to face
There is no dearth of those who discourse on
Him
Millions give millions upon millions of sermons
He ceaselessly gives, the recipients may tire
For eons, He has sustained the creation
By His command, He ordains all
O Nanak, He Himself remains in eternal bliss.

He is true, true is His name
Infinite the expressions of devotion
All creation begs boons and He bestows
What should we offer Him
For a glimpse of His court?
What words do we utter
To earn his love?
Meditate, in the ambrosial hours of dawn
On his true Name.
By good actions is the human form attained
By God's grace, the door to salvation
Know this Nanak: the Almighty is all

Neither can he be installed nor created
The Immaculate one is self-existent
Those who serve Him are honoured
O Nanak, sing the praise of His endless virtue

Sing and hear His praise, with His love in your
heart
Shedding pain, go home with bliss
The Guru's word is the Divine word,
And the true scripture,
And knowledge that He is all pervasive,
The Lord is all deities—Shiva, Vishnu, Brahma,
Parvati, Lakshmi, Saraswati.
Even if I know Him
I cannot describe the ineffable
My Master has enlightened me:
There is one Creator of all beings
This I should not forget.

If I please Him, it is my holy bath
Without His approval, what good is bathing?
Without good action, no one has obtained a
thing
But absorbing one thought of the Guru
Enriches the mind with gems, jewels, rubies
My Master has enlightened me:
There is one creator of all beings
This I should not forget.

Were a man to live for the four ages
And ten times more,
Were he to walk the nine continents

And gather followers,
Were he to have fame and praise
Of the whole world,
Without the grace of God
No one would care for him;
A worm amongst worms,
Accused even by sinners;
Nanak, the Divine being
Makes the non-virtuous virtuous,
None though can bestow virtue on Him

Listening to His Name, man equals
Siddhas, pirs, spiritual heroes, yogis,
Revealed are the mysteries of the earth,
The supporting bull and the heavens,
Of the continents, the worlds, the nether-worlds
Listening to His Name
Man is beyond death's reach
O Nanak, His devotees are ever in bliss
Listening to His Name
Destroys sorrows and sins
Listening to His Name
The seeker becomes Shiva, Brahma, Indra
Listening to His Name
Even the evil sing the Lord's praise
Listening to His Name
Man acquires true knowledge of esoteric powers

And comprehends all the scriptures
O Nanak, His devotees are ever in bliss
Listening to His Name
Destroys sorrows and sins

Listening to His Name
Brings Truth, contentment, Divine knowledge,
Listening to His Name
Equals bathing at the sixty-eight holy places
Listening and studying His Name
Bestows honour on the seeker
Listening to His Name
Fixes easily the mind in meditation
O Nanak, His devotees are ever in bliss
Listening to His Name
Destroys sorrows and sins

Asa Di Var

This long composition that forms part of the Adi Granth
is sung in the early hours of the morning. It is one of the
three compositions of Guru Nanak in a popular folk
form of Punjab, the var or heroic ballad, the others being
Majh di Var and *Malar di Var*. It consists of *chakkas*,
pauris and shlokas. The chakkas which form the
beginnings are the work of the fourth Guru, Ram Das.
There are twenty-four pauris and sixty shlokas, fifteen
of which were written by Guru Angad. The shlokas set

the context for the pauris, which form the core of the composition. The pauris praise God, the Guru and the true gurmukh.

In the *Asa di Var*, Guru Nanak emphasizes that the ultimate reality is one. This immortal creator, self-existent, creates all and watches over his creation ceaselessly. God is all-pervasive and only He is truly fearless. Man should follow the spiritual path and do God's will. Nanak criticizes social and administrative injustice as well as empty religious ritualism and blind superstition. He condemns formalism of all sorts and exposes the hypocrisy of religion as it was generally practised. He commends the religion of realization, the life of service, lived truthfully and the meditation of the name of God. There is a code of conduct that man needs to follow, that of truth and truthful living. Man must overcome his ego, cultivate humility and practise what he preaches. To attain this path, he needs the guidance of a guru. But great care has to exercised in choosing one's guru for false prophets abound. Only with the help of the true guru, who comes one's way with the grace of God, can salvation be attained and the soul unite with its maker.

The var is a beautiful piece of poetry, inspiring and rich. Abundant in spiritual content, yet full of sharp metaphors taken from daily life and told in the everyday language of Punjabi, it is a powerful composition meant for everyone, a thought that is reinforced by the fact that it is in a popular folk form. On reading it, one is lifted into a different spiritual realm that leaves behind superstition and blind belief and moves towards the fundamental verities of existence.

Shlok:

> A hundred times a day
> I sacrifice myself unto my Guru
> Who without delay
> Made Gods of men.

Shlok:

> O Nanak, those who forfeit the Lord
> Thinking themselves clever,
> They shall be discarded like false sesame
> In the reaped field
> Says Nanak: those left in the field
> Have no caretaker
> The wretches bear fruit and flower
> Yet carry within themselves only ash.

Pauri:

> The Lord created Himself
> Himself gave His name
> Then He created His creation
> And seated, beheld it in delight.

Thou yourself are the Giver and Doer
Pleased, you give and show mercy.
You are all-knowing
You give and take life with a word.
And seated, you behold your creation in delight.

The *Asa di Var* contains Guru Nanak's teachings
on the place of women in the world:

Within a woman conceived,
Of a woman born,
With a woman betrothed and married.
With a woman are sustained friendships
Through a woman, life goes on,
When a wife dies, one seeks another,
With woman man is bound,
Why call her bad then,
Who gives birth to Kings
From a woman is woman born,
Without her there is none.
Nanak, only the true Lord
Is beyond a woman

The mouth that praises
Is fortunate and beautiful
Nanak: such faces shall be radiant in the Lord's
court.

Siddha Gosht

During his travels, Nanak held discussions on several occasions with the holy men—Siddhas, yogis, sufi dervishes—who dominated the religious landscape those days. Notable among the yogis with whom Nanak interacted were the followers of Gorakhnath, the *kanphala* sect.

The two main discourses between Nanak and the Siddhas were held on Sumer Parbat, or Mount Kailash, and at Achal near Batala during the Shivratri fair. The message of the discourses is not a condemnation of yoga but a striving towards the true meaning of yogic principles and philosophy, shorn of ritualism and superstition and practised without renunciation. As against the practice of hathayoga, the Guru preached sahajyoga as the path to true spiritual attainment. Sahaj, or the balanced philosophy of life, enriched by prayer, meditation and devotion leads to the awareness of the divine in all creation. In *Siddha Gosht*, Guru Nanak elucidates the principles of Gurmat (The Guru's Philosophy): the concepts of the Word, Truth, the Guru, God's grace and so on. Nanak also enunciates his idea of *jivan-mukta* or the one who finds salvation in life itself and does not have to wait for death. This bani also expatiates on the idea of *simran* and the concepts of Gurmukh (the spiritual man) and Manmukh (the egocentric person), the first attuned towards God and the other towards his own self.

The discourses with the Siddhas are in the form of a dialogue, a question and answer examination of intellectual truths. The *Siddha Gosht* contains this dialogue in seventy-three verses, each of six lines and set in the musical measure of Ramkali. This bani of Nanak is usually regarded as one of the most thoughtful, symbolic and mature of his compositions, all the more so as it utilizes technical yogic vocabulary. It is also notable for the fact that the entire dialogue is conducted not antagonistically but in a spirit of humility, intellectual inquiry and mutual respect, free of rancour and steeped in tolerance. Here are some excerpts:

Said Charpat: O Nanak, the detached one, answer me truly.
Nanak: The one who asks that, himself knows. What can I answer him?
Truly speaking, how can I answer you, you who think that he has already reached the yonder shore.

Like the lotus is unaffected in water,
A duck swimming against the current is dry,
Similarly, with the mind on the Divine utterances
And repeating His Name, we cross the terrible

ocean of the world.

He who lives detached, enshrining the Lord in
his mind
Without desire in the midst of desire,
Sees and shows the Inaccessible and
Incomprehensible
Of him Nanak is a slave.

Say the Yogis:
Who is unmanifest? Who is emancipated?
Who is united within and without?
Who is he who comes and goes?
Who is he who pervades the three worlds?

Says Nanak:
The all pervasive is unmanifest
The spiritual man is free
He too is united within and without with the
Name
The self-centred man comes and goes
Nanak, His follower knows that He pervades
the three worlds.

Say the Yogis:
What is the origin of life? What faith
predominates the time?

Who is thy Guru, whose disciple are you?
Uttering whose discourse do you remain
unique?
Listen to what we say, O Nanak child.
Tell us of this discourse. How does the Lord
ferry man across the terrible ocean?

Says Nanak:
The breath is the beginning; the True Lord
hold's sway
The Lord my Guru, I his disciple love his
meditation
The discourse of the Ineffable One makes me
unique
O Nanak, the Cherisher of the world through
the ages is my Guru.
Unique is the Lord and meditating on His
discourse
His follower crosses the terrible ocean
And quenches the fire of his ego.

Listen O Yogi, to the quintessence of Divine
discourse
Without the Name, there is no yoga.
Those touched by the Name are intoxicated day
and night
Through the Name, they find peace.

Through the Name is all revealed
Through the Name comes understanding
Without the Name, many disguise themselves
Misled by the Lord himself.
From the True Lord is the Name attained
And then one knows the true yoga.
O Nanak, reflect in thy mind and see
There is no salvation without the Name.

You alone know Your size and estimation
What can anyone else explain?
You Yourself are hidden, and revealed
And Yours are all the joys
Many seekers, accomplished ones, spiritual
teachers,
And many disciples wander in Thy search, by
Thy command
Beseech thee for thy Name, and are granted;
O Lord, for thy vision I sacrifice myself.
The imperishable One has staged this play
His true follower understands
O Nanak, He alone pervades all worlds
There is no other.

Babar Vani

Guru Nanak's *Babar Vani* is the composition of protest
at the invasion of Babar and the suffering inflicted on

innocent citizens, particularly the womenfolk. In four shabads, three of which are set to the Raga Asa and the fourth to Raga Tilang, Nanak pours forth the reaction of not just an eyewitness but also of a philosophical sage, a visionary and a poet. The suffering of humankind, the shortcomings of that age, the profligacy of India's rulers at that time, the nature of the divine will and the suffering that mankind has to endure when the cosmic principles on which the world rests are ignored, are all brought out in these compositions renowned for their truth, spiritual insight and literary beauty.

> As God's Word comes to me
> So I speak, O Lalo.
>
> He (Babar) has charged from Kabul
> With the wedding party of sin
> And demands gifts by force, O Lalo.
>
> Modesty and righteousness
> Are in hiding
> Falsehood is in command, O Lalo.
>
> The Qazis and Brahmins
> Have had their day,
> Satan reads the marriage vows, O Lalo.

Muslim women read the Quran
In suffering
Call on God, O Lalo.

And Hindu women
Of caste high and low
Suffer the same fate, O Lalo.

O Nanak, paeans of blood are sung
And anointment is not by saffron
But blood, O Lalo.

Nanak sings the virtues of the Lord
In this city of corpses
And utters this truth:

The One who created men
And gave them joys
Beholds them in His solitude.

He is True,
True His verdict
And true His justice

—Raga Tilang

They with the beautiful tresses
Sacred vermillion in their partings,

Their heads are now shorn with scissors
And dust chokes their throats
They who lived in palaces
No longer can even sit outside
Praise to thee O Lord, praise,
O Primal Lord, none knows your limits,
Endlessly, You behold Yourself in diverse forms.

When they were married,
Their bridegrooms handsome beside them,
They came seated in palanquins,
And adorned in ornaments of ivory,
Welcoming waters greeted them
And glittering fans comforted them from close,
Riches were gifted as they sat
And riches when they stood,
They ate coconuts and dates
And took pleasure on comfortable beds;
Ropes now are around their necks
Their pearl strings are broken.
The wealth and youthful beauty
That gave them joy, are now their enemy;
The soldiers have been ordered, and
Dishonouring them, they take them away.

                —Raga Asa